Wychwood and Cornbury

An old oak tree in Cornbury Park.

Wychwood and Cornbury

Charles Tyzack

Based on Vernon J. Watney's
Cornbury and the Forest of Wychwood (1910)

THE WYCHWOOD PRESS

Our books may be ordered from bookshops or (post free) from
Jon Carpenter Publishing, Alder House, Market Street, Charlbury OX7 3PH
01608 811969

e-mail: wychwood@joncarpenter.co.uk

Credit card orders should be phoned or faxed to 01689 870437 or
01608 811969

Please ask for our free catalogue

First published in 2003 by
The Wychwood Press
an imprint of Jon Carpenter Publishing
Alder House, Market Street, Charlbury, Oxfordshire OX7 3PH

ISBN 1 902279 04 2

Printed in England by J.W. Arrowsmith Ltd

Contents

List of illustrations

Maps and plans

Illustration credits

All the illustrations are from Vernon J. Watney, *Cornbury and the Forest of Wychwood*, except the following:

Charlbury Museum, 56, 99, 148

Charles Keighley, 107, 116

Ron Prew, 80, 130, 140, 141 (2)

Lord Rotherwick, 142 (2), 146

Beryl Schumer, 7

W. Shaw Sparrow, *The British Home of Today* (1904), 134, 136

Alan Spicer, 120

Roy Townsend, 131

The Author, 14, 25, 50, 66, 112, 122

Preface

In 1910 Vernon Watney, who had bought the Cornbury Estate in 1901, published his *Cornbury and the Forest of Wychwood*, which has been seen ever since as the main source book for information about the history of Wychwood Forest and Cornbury Park. It is an invaluable work, but one that is not easy either to find or to read. It was published privately, by Hatchards of Piccadilly, in an edition of only 100 copies. Physically it is a magnificent book, printed on hand-made paper with wide margins, bound in heavy boards and red leather, with a fine collection of sepia photographs printed on thin card and protected by tissue paper. Those lucky enough to own a copy are understandably reluctant to let it out of their possession.

With a modesty that seems characteristic of the man, Watney refers to himself as 'a compiler' rather than an author, and in his book he has collected together, it seems, all the references he could find to Wychwood and Cornbury, and those who have lived there, over nearly a millennium. Entries in Pipe Rolls and Exchequer Accounts, Parliamentary Reports, proceedings of Forest Courts, State Papers, wills, diaries, private and official letters, together with lengthy extracts from the recently published *Dictionary of National Biography* – all these make up the substance of Watney's book. But this material remains relatively undigested, and he did little to shape it into a narrative. He was also fascinated by genealogy, and his book includes a four-page table listing the tenants, occupiers and owners of Wychwood, Cornbury, and the Manor of Langley, and an astonishingly complex fold-out chart stretching from the twelfth to the twentieth century, to illustrate how these various people are related to each other. He includes much material about them which has no connection with Wychwood or Cornbury, though often interesting for its own sake. In addition to its fourteen chapters, the book contains twenty-three appendices, and separate essays by other hands on the Architecture of Cornbury House, and the Botany of Wychwood Forest and Cornbury Park.

So, even if a copy of *Cornbury and the Forest of Wychwood* can be found, it is not a very approachable work. In presenting it to the general reader of today, I have tried to give it some narrative shape and have left out most of the material that does not relate to the locality. At the same time I have included the results of research that has been done over the years since 1910. The first six chapters are based mainly on Watney, though not for the most part using his words; the last two consist largely of new material, and take the story up to 1966, the year when Watney's son Oliver died, and the estate passed out of the hands of the family.

Only rarely does Watney name his sources. His book contains, he writes, 'but few references to authorities, for such references would have been, by their number, wearisome to the casual, and for the most part unnecessary to the professed, student of local history. No opportunity,' he continues, 'has been wittingly lost of following the old advice, "Verify your quotations"...' But this has to be taken for the most part on trust. I too have not wished to load down the book with footnotes, but I have tried on important matters to mention my source in the text, and further reference to the bibliography should point the reader in the right direction.

I am most grateful to the students of local history, both 'casual' and 'professed', and others who have helped me in the preparation of this book. First of all I must thank Beryl Schumer, the doyenne of Wychwood Studies, for introducing me to many valuable sources, and giving up time to discuss Watney and Wychwoodery with me. I am especially grateful to her for allowing me to use unpublished results of her recent research. The present owner of Cornbury, Lord Rotherwick, has kindly allowed me access to a Watney photograph album, and to use several of the pictures there. Ann Buckmaster has drawn the maps of Wychwood on pp. x - xiii. Margaret Merry and Roy Shadbolt have provided fascinating details about life at Cornbury in the Watney era; and I would also like to thank Simon Drummond-Hay, David Eddershaw, Belinda Flitter (Wychwood Project), Lois Hey, Gillian Naish and Ron Prew of the Charlbury Museum, and the staff of the Centre for Oxfordshire Studies, and the Oxfordshire County Record Office, for information and assistance of various kinds.

Finally I would like to thank my Publisher, Jon Carpenter, for suggesting to me a project which has given me so much instruction and enjoyment.

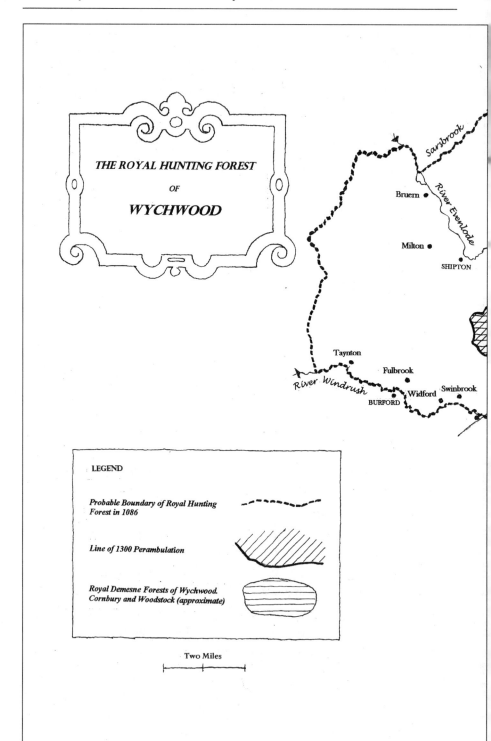

THE ROYAL HUNTING FOREST

OF

WYCHWOOD

Bruern

Milton

SHIPTON

River Evenlode

Sarsbrook

Taynton

Fulbrook

River Windrush

Widford   Swinbrook

BURFORD

LEGEND

Probable Boundary of Royal Hunting
Forest in 1086

Line of 1300 Perambulation

Royal Demesne Forests of Wychwood,
Cornbury and Woodstock (approximate)

Two Miles

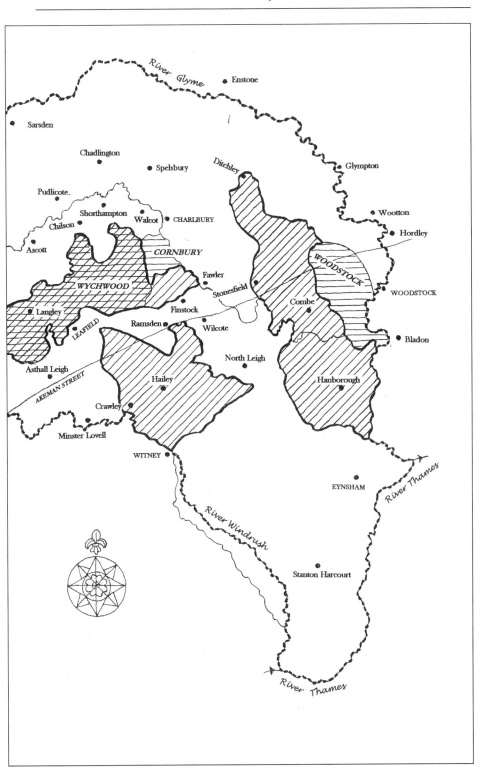

River Glyme

Enstone

Sarsden

Chadlington

Spelsbury

Ditchley

Glympton

Pudlicote.

Shorthampton

Walcot

CHARLBURY

Wootton

Chilson

Hordley

Ascott

CORNBURY

WOODSTOCK

Fawler

Stonesfield

WOODSTOCK

WYCHWOOD

Combe

Langley

Finstock

Bladon

LEAFIELD

Ramsden

Wilcote

Asthall Leigh

North Leigh

AKEMAN STREET

Hailey

Hanborough

Crawley

Minster Lovell

WITNEY

EYNSHAM

River Thames

River Windrush

Stanton Harcourt

River Thames

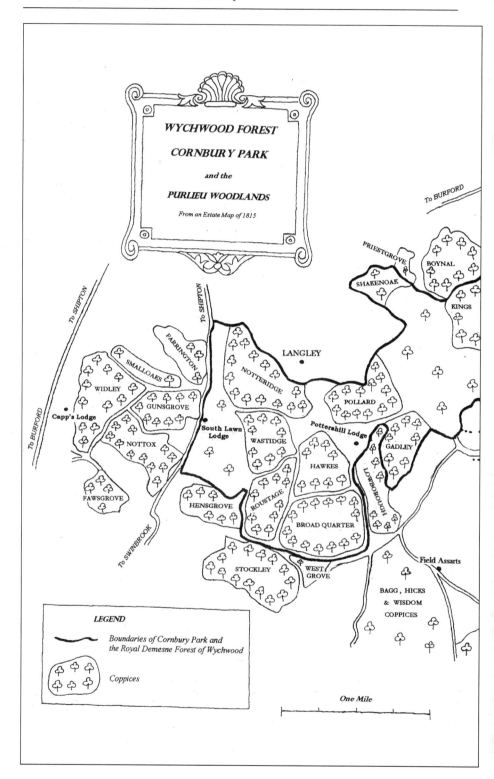

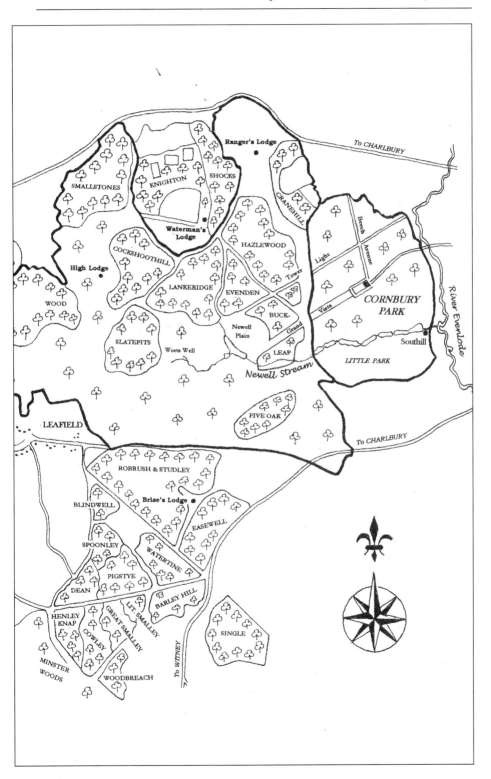

Ground plan of Cornbury House in 1910, from Vernon Watney, *Cornbury and the Forest of Wychwood.*

Wychwood Forest

It is in the *Domesday Book* of 1086 that we find the earliest mention of Cornbury, as one of 'the demesne forests of the King in Shotover, Stowood, Woodstock, Cornbury, and Wychwood'. In a few early documents 'Cornbury' is called 'Acornberry', and given the dominance of oak trees in the area Vernon Watney understandably thought this was the origin of the name. However, Margaret Gelling in *The Place-Names of Oxfordshire* derives the syllable 'corn' from 'crane' – Cornbury was a fortification ('bury') haunted by cranes. For 'Wychwood', Watney mentions an attractive but fanciful derivation from the Welsh 'hwcha', a sow, suggesting that the people who lived there were swineherds attracted by the 'acorn berries'. However, 'Wychwood' almost certainly comes from the name of a Saxon tribe, the Hwicce, who lived in east Gloucestershire in the seventh century. Perhaps their territory extended into what is now west Oxfordshire, but, as John Blair has pointed out, the wood may instead have been an outlying resource within the land of their neighbours, the Gewisse, and thus specifically referred to as the 'Hwicce's wood'. The first written reference is found in a Charter of 841, which shows that it then extended north as far as Spelsbury.

Evidence of human activity in the Wychwood area, however, goes back much further. The oldest structure is a Neolithic long-chambered barrow in the western part of the present-day Forest near Churchill Copse, and there are many ancient earthworks, such as Knollbury, near Chadlington, and Lyneham Camp. Grim's Ditch, a pre-Roman series of earthworks, starts near the river Glyme, and runs through Ditchley and Cornbury round to North Leigh. The Romans built numerous villas, most notably at Shakenoak, North Leigh, Fawler and Ditchley; and Akeman Street passes through the Forest. Recently a Roman military encampment has been identified within Cornbury Park itself. In Saxon times it became part of the Kingdom of Mercia, and the seventh-century Bishop of Mercia, St. Diuma, is said to have been buried at Charlbury. By the time of Edward the Confessor Wychwood had become part of the royal demesne, together with the other forests mentioned in Domesday, and after the Conquest they passed to William I.

Historically, the term 'Wychwood Forest' is used in two very different ways. Firstly, it refers to the royal demesne forest that had belonged to the Saxon Kings, and which stretched westwards from the boundaries of Cornbury as far as the present Shipton-Swinbrook road, by South Lawn. This land belonged to the King, and some of it remains part of the Crown Estate to this day. But 'Wychwood Forest' is also the name of the much larger Royal Hunting Forest created by William I, and made subject to Norman Forest Law. The boundary of this Forest would vary a good deal over the centuries, but under William it probably ran along the rivers Glyme, the lower Evenlode, the Thames, and the Windrush as far as the Oxfordshire-Gloucestershire border; then along the county boundary and the Sarsbrook, back to the source of the Glyme. This included the three royal forests of Woodstock, Cornbury, and Wychwood, and the royal manor of Shipton; but by far the larger part was held by barons, bishops, abbots, and other greater or lesser manorial lords. Forest Law, however, imposed severe restrictions on what they could do on their own land. This Law was distinct from the Common Law; it derived entirely from the arbitrary will of the King, and it could not be challenged in the ordinary courts. Forest Law was deeply resented, and the Anglo-Saxon Chronicle records its introduction as one of William's most oppressive actions.

Wychwood, in both senses, may have been called a 'Forest', but this does not mean that it was all woodland. It also included village open fields, sheepwalks, ridings, heathland and uncultivated waste. Recent research suggests that a good deal of land in this area had already been cleared by the late Iron Age, and not in Saxon or Norman times as was once believed. Indeed, it may have been the collapse of Roman power in Britain and the consequent decline in agriculture, which led to the area becoming more wooded. For much was indeed 'forest covert' – covered by large trees, mostly oak and ash. There were also maples; and hawthorn, holly, crab and ivy are mentioned as food for deer. Beeches were probably not introduced until the seventeenth century. It is possible that much of the woodland was already managed, and divided into coppices, before the Conquest, as the shape of the coppices often reflects the boundaries of manorial woods.

The inhabitants of the manors surrounding the demesne Forest of Wychwood (the 'Forest' in its more limited sense) held rights of common pasture there, on payment of the appropriate dues. We have no detailed record from any date earlier than 1792, but it is likely that the Parliamentary Commissioners' Report of that year describes practices already many centuries old. The rights would not have been granted under Forest Law, so they probably go back to Saxon times. In 1792 the following manors enjoyed the right to pasture horses and horned cattle (except for oxen): Ascott Doyley, Chilson, Pudlicot, Shorthampton, Walcot, Finstock, Ramsden, Leafield, Langley, Asthall, Asthall Leigh, Minster Lovell, Swinbrook, Fulbrook, Taynton (Painsfarm), and Widford. In addition Leafield, Langley and Shorthampton could pasture sheep on the open sheepwalks. During the 'fence month' – two weeks each side of Midsummer Day – when the deer were fawning, all animals had to be removed, and no carts could pass through the Forest. Any common rights that may have existed in Cornbury had disappeared by 1270.

The purpose of the Forest Law was to preserve the deer for the King to hunt. Under William I almost a quarter of England became Royal Hunting Forest, and the Norman monarchs were all passionate huntsmen. William I 'loved the stags as if he had been their father,' William II died on the hunting field, and of Henry I it was written by a disapproving chronicler, William of Newburgh, that 'he cared for the wild animals more than was right, and in public punishment he made too little distinction between one who killed a deer, and one who killed a man.' Only the King, or those with his authority, could hunt the Royal Beasts of the Chase: red, roe and fallow deer, and wild boar. Punishment for poaching was extreme – blinding, castration or death.

Other animals – hare, fox, cat, badger, marten – could be hunted, but only with a special permit, as hunting dogs were not normally allowed in the Forest. Forest dwellers who owned dogs had to have them 'lawed' – three toes cut from a forefoot to prevent them chasing deer.

To provide covert and forage for the deer the wood was also protected, and those who held land covered by Forest Law could only cut down trees

or clear land with royal permission. This made it much harder for manorial lords to develop the economic potential of their holdings. It is notable
that more Forest Laws refer to the preservation of wood than of deer, and
offences 'against the vert' (for example, felling trees) were always more
numerous than offences 'against the venison'.

There is little evidence of how Forest Law was administered in the
Norman period, but many documents have survived from the thirteenth
century and the reign of Henry III to tell us about the complex life of the
Forest and its administration, as it had developed by that time. The chief
Officer of a Forest was the Forester or Warden, appointed directly by the
King. In Wychwood, as in many other forests, the post was hereditary, but
the Forester could still be suspended from office if he failed to carry out his
duties properly. The Forester, also known in later times as the Lieutenant,
Keeper, or Ranger, appointed sub-foresters, woodwards and others to help
him in his duties. He had the responsibility for day-to-day management of
the Forest, for carrying out royal commands, and for ensuring that Forest
Law was observed. He had a particular duty to care for the demesne forests,
but also had to ensure that nowhere in the wider Hunting Forest were trees
cut down without his approval. He also had the far more dangerous task of
arresting poachers. These could include clerics, since the benefit of clergy
did not apply under Forest Law, and a Forest so close to Oxford attracted
numerous marauding clerks.

One group of clergy, however, were welcome: the 'hermits', to be found
in Royal Forests throughout the country. These were not individuals
seeking peace and solitude for the good of their souls, but priests who lived
in a forest to say mass for the forest workers, 'so that they can remain in the
Forest for the safe keeping of the King's beasts'. In 1232 there was a
hermitage at 'Louebury' (probably Lowbarrow, just south of Leafield); in
that year the Forester was ordered to ensure that the chaplain Lucian
succeeded to it on the death of the present hermit, Ernald, to whom he
ministered. In 1270 'the hermitage which is within the King's Forest of
Wychwood', possibly the same one, was given by the King to the Hospital
of St. John at Lechlade, whose Prior would now have the duty of appointing
a hermit. In 1403 a hermit called Simon Kirton was given permission to
enclose two crofts with hedges and ditches at 'Newelme', which was probably on the edge of Newell Plain. There was also a small monastic site
called Pheleley, or Felelegh, which may have served the same purpose as a

hermitage. This was to the south of Ditchley Park, near Spurnell's Well, which may have been a religious site back in the Iron Age.

Apart from the Forester there was a whole hierarchy of other Forest officials with various responsibilities, which included keeping an eye on the Forester himself. The highest Forest officers in the land, first appointed by Henry II, were the Justices in Eyre, of whom there were two for the whole country – one for forests north of the River Trent and one for those to the south. These justices presided over courts – the Forest Eyres, or Pleas – which were supposed to be held in each county once every three years, and which dealt with all the major offences against Forest Law. Then there were the Verderers, two for each forest, who held Courts of Attachment, or Swanimote Courts, meeting several times a year, and dealing with lesser offences. For example, cutting down a sapling would be dealt with by the Verderers, but the cutting of a green oak could only be punished at the Eyre. The Verderers were local gentry, elected by freeholders in the County Court, but answerable to the Justice. Agistors, four for each county and again chosen from the local gentry, regulated the use of the common land for pasture and collected the dues, which they passed on to the Sheriff. 'Herbage' was paid for the pasturing of domestic animals, and 'pannage' for pigs. These would be let in to the forest at Michaelmas to graze on the mast (including acorns). First the Agistors would have to check on the mast crop that year, and regulate the number of pigs accordingly. In some years there was no crop, so none were let in. At Martinmas they were brought out, and pannage was then levied – in Wychwood this consisted of one pig in every three.

The work of the Agistors was generally accepted, and agistment under one name or another continued for as long as the Forest itself. But the task of the final group of Forest officers was widely resented. These were the Regarders, of whom there were twelve for each county – again, local gentry, but chosen by the Sheriff. Every three years, before the Forest Pleas were held, a 'Regard of the Forest' took place, during which all offences against the Forest Laws would be recorded, for presentation to the Court. The Regarders' instructions were written down in the Chapters of the Regard, the earliest surviving version of which dates from 1229. These contain a series of detailed questions about land, acreage, crops, new clearances or 'assarted' land, and who was responsible for them. Every tree-stump had to be accounted for; honey had to be viewed and the right to it determined – was it the King's or the manorial lord's? They had to enquire who owned bows and crossbows, and to check that all dogs had been lawed. They had to inspect forges and mines, and any river-harbours from which timber might be shipped. They had to pay special attention to the demesne lands and see that they were properly kept. Landowners within a forest were allowed to cut wood for their own use – this was known as 'estover' – but only with the Forester's approval. If they cut down more they could be accused of 'wasting' the land, and the wasted land would be enclosed (effectively confiscated) until the trees had grown back. There was a definition of 'waste' – if you stood on one tree-stump and could see six others, then the land was 'wasted'. If the landowners cleared their land altogether and grew crops there, then the crop would be taxed. It is not surprising that the Regard was so disliked, and that many tried to have their land taken 'out of Regard', or claimed that it should never have been in Regard in the first place.

Forest Law received definitive form with Henry II's Assize of Woodstock in 1184, which laid down the details of administration and how offences were to be punished. Henry reasserted the full severity of the Norman law, which had grown slacker under Stephen; but, enthusiastic huntsman though he was, he also realised the economic potential of the forests. Death and maiming were still prescribed as punishments, but in practice could always be replaced by fines. Manorial lords were willing to pay substantial sums to have their land removed from the Regard; they could also be allowed to clear and cultivate land on payment of a perpetual rent dependent on the crops grown – a shilling an acre for wheat, sixpence for oats.

During the thirteenth century the economic benefits of the forests to the royal government became ever more apparent, and the sale of underwood and timber trees from the demesne woodlands were a major source of income for Henry III. Woodland management must have required some form of coppicing, to protect the young shoots and saplings from damage. Probably already, as in the later years of which we have record, a coppice would be cut every twenty years or so; it then had to be fenced off for seven years to keep out deer and pasturing cattle. The fence was usually placed on top of an earth bank, with a ditch in front, to make it more secure against the deer. When it was cut a number of oaks within each coppice would be preserved for timber. An Act for the Preservation of Timber in 1543

Coppice with standards in the Wychwood area today

decreed that 12 'standels' or saplings per acre should be kept, and this may well reflect the 'best practice' of earlier years.

When the underwood was sold it was divided into 40 braids, or breadths, an acre, each measuring one pole in length by four in width. No one was allowed to buy wholesale, and it was offered in the first instance to the poorer tenants. Some figures for sales of underwood survive from the later Middle Ages. In 1436 the underwood from one coppice was sold for £26. 17s. 11d; the cost of refencing the coppice came to £16. 1s. 11d., leaving a tidy profit. The situation was different a hundred years later in 1535, when the sale of 28 acres of underwood only brought in £4. 2s. 3d., and the refencing cost £9. 9s. If this last figure is typical it helps to explain the later decline in the condition of the Forest, as it ceased to be economically viable to secure the coppices properly against the deer and cattle.

It was as much his recognition of the forests' economic value as a love of hunting that led Henry II to add a further fifteen manors to Wychwood, so that it then stretched to the Thames in the south, the Cherwell in the east, and along the Giiling brook to the Warwickshire border in the north. Richard I was rarely in England, but King John sought to make the maximum profit from the forests. He imposed heavy fines for petty offences, and in 1208 ordered all buildings, fences and ditches within the forests removed, even though they had been there for decades. It is not surprising that the Forest was one of the matters addressed in Magna Carta, by which John was forced to remove the areas that he had added to the forests, and to promise that all 'ill customs' should be enquired into and abolished.

When Henry III came to the throne he was still a child, and the barons took advantage of this to issue a Charter of the Forest in 1217, which greatly clarified Forest Law and its administration. Henry II's additions were removed, and the boundaries of 1154, the year of Henry's coronation, restored. Penalties of death and maiming were abolished. Free men were allowed to agist their own woods and have their own pannage, to cultivate their own land within a forest, and construct mills and dig ditches on it. Bishops and lords were allowed to take one or two deer for themselves whenever they travelled through a forest. The Charter still left the boundaries uncertain, however, especially of those areas that had been forest under Henry I, but had been taken out under Stephen. So the following year orders were given for regular 'perambulations' to determine their true extent.

When Henry III came of age in 1227 he had the right to cancel all charters issued during his minority. He did not cancel the Forest Charter, but did reopen the question of forest boundaries, cancelling earlier perambulations and ordering new ones. In 1228 he tried to take back land afforested by Henry II, but this met with strong opposition. In 1237, in need of funds to pursue his war against the barons, he reaffirmed the Charter of 1217; but the forest remained a matter of political contention throughout the century, and the effective bounds probably varied according to whether the King or the barons were in the ascendant. These conflicts may have affected Wychwood less than other forests, since Henry III was particularly fond of Woodstock and often stayed there, taking a direct interest in the management of the estate. More than elsewhere, his word would have been law.

During Edward I's reign the King needed funds for his military campaigns, and much forest land was cleared for cultivation, and the timber sold for profit. Towards the end of the thirteenth century he was fighting on two fronts, in France and Scotland. William Wallace had won the battle of Stirling Bridge, and the barons took advantage of the King's weakness to demand a new perambulation of all the forests in England. Its declared aim, like that of previous perambulations, was to determine where the boundaries had been in 1154, at the time of Henry II's coronation. Reluctantly Edward agreed, and the perambulation took place in 1300. In Wychwood it was undertaken by three Justices, together with 24 Oxfordshire gentry acting as jurors. A group of Oxfordshire jurors back in 1217 had claimed that only the royal demesne lands had been forest in the days of Stephen, and this was now confirmed.

The 1300 perambulation removed from the Royal Hunting Forest of Wychwood about two-thirds of the total – in effect, everything that did not already belong to the King, apart from the Bishop of Winchester's estate north of Witney. The jurors ignored earlier settlements and declared that all these areas had been newly afforested by Henry II or his sons. When asked for the sources of their information, they referred to the tales of their ancestors and the common talk of the country. Three discontinuous areas now made up the sharply reduced Wychwood Forest. One consisted of Ditchley and Woodstock, together with the royal manors of Wootton, Combe, Stonesfield, Bladon and Hanborough; the second was the royal demesne forests of Cornbury and Wychwood; and the third the Bishop of Winchester's lands forming a triangle between Leafield, North Leigh and Witney.

The same thing happened in Royal Forests throughout England. The King was enraged and appealed to the Pope, who found in his favour, and the perambulations were cancelled by an Ordinance of the Forest in 1306. The conflict over the forest continued, however, and was exacerbated by Edward II, who made his favourite Piers Gaveston Justice of the Forests, and granted him the right to appoint the verderers, hitherto the prerogative of the local gentry. Only in 1327, when Edward II had been deposed and murdered, did Queen Isabella formally accept the 1300 Perambulation, and the question of the boundaries was apparently settled.

However, recent research by Beryl Schumer suggests that the story is less straightforward. Various Forest Inquisitions during the reign of Edward III still deal with assarting and coppicing in areas outside the Royal demesne lands – for example in Charlbury and Eynsham – and many of the jurors are recorded as living within the Forest bounds. Only free men could serve as jurors, and there would be few such living on the royal lands. Edward III did take back some forest lands in Surrey and Dorset, and while there is no record of this happening in Wychwood, it seems that the King reasserted his authority over lands that had been signed away by his mother, or at least over the wooded areas. Some fifteenth-century records also refer to woods supposedly disafforested in 1327 as lying 'within the metes and bounds' of Wychwood. It now seems likely that the Royal Hunting Forest retained a shadowy existence until the seventeenth century, with monarchs occasionally trying, and usually failing, to make their power over this wider area more effective.

But the forests were certainly of less interest to the royal government than they had been. With an increase in trade new sources of income had appeared: customs duties could be levied and merchants taxed. Income from the forests was less important, and the forest administration gently declined. Forest Law remained in force, but the Forest Eyres were held less frequently, and not at all by the later fourteenth century. How order was kept is not wholly clear; maybe the Forester dispensed summary justice, or the Attachment Courts gave themselves greater powers. The post of Forester itself became a valuable means of royal patronage, and was increasingly seen less as a responsibility than a source of profit. The Royal Forests of England had entered upon five hundred years of neglect and slow decay.

Hereditary Foresters

The family that held the office of hereditary Forester of Wychwood until the mid-fourteenth century claimed to have held it since the Conquest, but this is questionable. Domesday tells us that the tenant of the five royal demesne forests in Oxfordshire (including Wychwood, Cornbury and Woodstock) was Rainald, who paid a fee of ten pounds a year to the King for the privilege. According to Domesday several Rainalds held land in Oxfordshire; the most probable candidate for the one who held the forests is a man who was tenant of Chadlington, and Ipsden in Buckinghamshire, and is also mentioned in connection with Stanton Harcourt. Presumably he was a Norman.

Nearly fifty years later, according to the Pipe Rolls of 1130-1, Baldwin Rasor renders ten pounds for the census of 'the forest of Oxfordshire', the same sum that Rainald had paid nearly fifty years earlier. From 1154-8 payments were made by Alan Rasor, presumably Baldwin's son. It may be that Baldwin was Rainald's descendant, as in 1279 the tenure of the forest was described as being 'de conquestu'. The Rasors have no known connection with Chadlington or Stanton Harcourt; however, from 1158 the payment is reduced to £7 per year, the remaining £3 being paid by a Richard de Camville for a forest area initially referred to as 'Corneberie', but later called the 'Forest of Stanton'.

From 1184 to 1194 Alan's son Richard paid the yearly fee for the forests; then for about 10 years the payment is in the names of various royal officials. This suggests that Richard had lost the custody of the Forest for some offence. He seems to have died about 1205, and in 1208 a 'Thomas de Langley' pays the fee; a later reference to him as 'son of Richard son of Alan' makes it clear that this is the same family under a new surname.

Thomas has taken his surname from the township of Langley, which had belonged to his uncle Roger son of Alan in 1196, and possibly earlier to Alan himself. However that may be, in the thirteenth century Langley was the base from which the Forest was ruled. Thomas held office until his death c.1240, to be succeeded by his brother William, whose descendants would be Foresters until the death of his great-great-grandson Sir Thomas de Langley in 1362.

The annual payments for the census of the Forest, which were made to the Exchequer every year until 1499, were all recorded under the heading of 'Cornbury'. Henry I was there about 1105, and several of his Charters are signed 'apud Cornberiam'. He may have built a hunting lodge there, and since one of the charters is witnessed by two bishops, a number of barons, and the King's brother-in-law, later King David of Scotland, it could have been a building of some size. But from then on Cornbury disappears from view for two centuries, apart from the annual entries in the Exchequer records.

Initially it seems that the Forester only looked after the demesne forests; but the accession of Henry II and his expansion of the Forest brought new arrangements in its wake. The two eastern forests of Stowood and Shotover were placed under another forester, but instead Alan Rasor was given responsibility for the oversight of Wychwood Forest in its wider sense, the whole Royal Hunting Forest.

Langley, which may have been held by the Rasors, and from which Thomas de Langley took his name, is not mentioned in Domesday, and there is no reference to it as a manor before 1259. The family also held land in Milton; and one of these estates (sources differ as to which) was held 'on the service' of carrying the King's horn whenever the King hunted in Wychwood. This was not the only quaint feudal custom associated with the Forest: there was a hide of land in Bletchingdon held of the King on the service of presenting a roast of pork (price threepence halfpenny) to the King, whenever he should hunt in Cornbury. Manor or no, Langley was the natural centre of the Forest administration. From here, one of the highest points in the Forest, the de Langleys could gaze for miles over the sheepwalks and woodlands of their baili-wick. Langley acquired royal connections as well: King John, who had been born at Woodstock, is said to have built a hunting lodge there, and

Edward I visited in 1281. Centuries later it would become a favourite resort of Tudor monarchs.

Thomas de Langley is first recorded as Forester in 1208, when he paid £22.15s into the Exchequer to cover the unpaid census of the Forest for the previous three and a quarter years. There were some doubts over the legality of his tenure, and in 1213, to ensure his rights, he promised to give King John 100 marks and 'a good palfrey'. The King also gave him 4 acres of land within the Forest – this may have been on the site of the present High Lodge. He was already far from a poor man: he had inherited the whole of Langley, and he also had houses, a mill, and land in Burford, Shipton, Milton and Crawley. The rights he possessed as hereditary Forester also gave him a good income. They included 'cheminage', the levying of road-tolls on people from outside the Forest, and most importantly the 'lop, top and bark' from all trees cut down within the Forest. He was also allowed the 'branch and breakage' – the branches and tops of trees uprooted by the wind. Oak bark in particular was a valuable product, and oaks were usually cut in late May, when the sap was rising and the bark could easily be stripped. Bark was used in tanning leather; tanning was an important occupation in both Witney and Burford, for which Wychwood deer and Cotswold sheep provided the raw materials.

By the thirteenth century, and especially by the reign of Henry III, there are numerous documents that can tell us something about the day-to-day responsibilities that fell to the de Langleys. Wood was the most valuable Forest product, used for building, fencing, firewood, and the making of charcoal, used in turn to fire the pottery kilns at Leafield; and many royal commands deal with the felling and transporting of trees. In 1231 Thomas was ordered to supply timber to make roof shingles for the King's Great Wardrobe at Woodstock, and the following year for rafters and joists for the porch and steps of the Great Chamber there. In 1246 the Chamber itself needed re-roofing and 140 oaks were felled for this purpose. But not all the wood was for the King's own use. In 1232 the Abbot of Bruern was allowed 10 oaks for the building of a church, and the Bishop of Cirencester received 40 oaks for the building of houses at Hensington, near Bladon. Two years later he was granted 60 rafters to build stables there. The Parson of Wootton was given 10 oaks from Pinsley Wood, in Hanborough, to build a tower for his church. Timber was also sent to the brethren of the Hospital

Riding between Buckleap and Hazelwood copses.

of St.John at Lechlade, and to the Archbishop of York for building a stable at Oddington. And there were smaller grants to lesser people: five oaks to John Beauchamp, one oak to Paul de Wincheles, and three oaks to Nicholas de Farenham.

Firewood was needed as well as building timber. The King and his court were often at Woodstock and needed to be fed and kept warm: in 1235 448 loads of firewood and 252 quarters of charcoal were taken from Cornbury to Woodstock for the King's use, and similar amounts over the next four years. In 1216 the Abbot of Bruern was given permission to send a third cart to the forest to collect firewood, in addition to the two he was already allowed; this grant being made by the King 'for the good of the souls of his father's ancestors'. And not only the powerful benefited: in 1234 Thomas was told to send a dry oak to the leper women of Woodstock, to be used for firewood.

The second major responsibility related to the deer and other game. Deer were required for the royal table, and would be sent around the country, either alive or dead and salted, to wherever the King was making his progress. Venison was also sent to royal relatives or favoured friends. These included Eleanor, Countess of Pembroke, the King's sister; Master Robert Oterinton; William de Ralegh; and Walter de Kirkham, Canon of Lincoln. In 1234 20 bucks were to be sent 'without delay' to Gilbert Marshall, Earl of Pembroke, for a feast to celebrate his knighting. In 1231 the nuns of

Godstow obtained a valuable favour from Henry III: a tithe of all deer taken in the Forest, whether by the King hunting in person or otherwise.

By the thirteenth century richer manorial lords were increasingly eager to create their own hunting parks. This meant that the land would be removed from the Regard, and commoners would lose their right to pasture. For this privilege the lords had to pay a large fine to the King. Then they needed to stock their new parks, and the King was ready to help, no doubt in return for a further payment. From Wychwood six does were sent to Robert de Harcourt, to stock his park at Bosworth, four does and one buck to Eva de Gray for her park at Standlake, five bucks and five does to Roger de Quency for his park at Chinnor. Not only deer were transferred: in 1217 Thomas was told to allow William de Brewere to take ten wild boars and ten trees from Wychwood, and in 1220 two boars were taken to the royal park at Havering, within Waltham Forest.

Every year the King would spend some time at Woodstock, and we can be sure that he hunted in the Forest. The name of the present Kingstanding Farm records a place where the monarch would stand to shoot at the deer as they were driven towards him. A document of 1312 tells us something of the forces that might be involved, even in the King's absence. The Forester of the time was ordered to help three of the King's yeomen to take six stags from the Forest, and the Sheriff of Oxford was to pay their wages. They would bring with them

> two *haericii* berners and four *haericii* veutrers, and two *daemericii* berners and two *daemericii* veutrers, and twenty-four *haericii* dogs and twenty-four coursing *daemericii* dogs and thirty greyhounds, to take the King's venison this present season in the forest of Wychwood, paying them from the present day of St. James during their stay in the bailiwick 12d a day each, 2d daily for each of the two *haericii* berners, 2d a day for each of the four *haericii* veutrers, 1½d a day for each of the said *daemericii* berners, and 2d a day for each of the said *daemericii* veutrers. He is also to provide the said yeomen with salt for the venison and with carriage for the same.

Berners were men in charge of running hounds, and veutrers in charge of greyhounds. *Daemericii* were buckhounds, and *haericii* harriers. It seems a lot of trouble for six stags.

Maintaining law and order within the Forest was another of the Forester's duties. He had to clear the land alongside the roads, to prevent robbers lurking under cover and waylaying travellers. Offences against the laws of vert and venison had to be 'presented', either to the Verderers' court, for minor offences, or to the triennial Forest Eyre. There must have been a small prison at Langley, for in 1233 Thomas was ordered to take the evil-doers he had in custody to Oxford Castle, to face trial. Poachers were mostly local villagers, but some were of higher rank. The Forester was specifically enjoined not to fear arresting poaching clerks. In 1256 Parson Geoffrey of Stonesfield was before the court for receiving clerks from Oxford, 'who were accustomed to take the Lord King's venison'; and in the 1290s Simon de Prewes, the parson of Great Tew, was fined one mark for poaching. In the 1250s all four sons of the Lord of Walcot, Savary, were found guilty. The inhabitants of Walcot were particularly troublesome: the Attachment Roll of 1245 records 113 offences against the vert, 62 of which had been committed by Walcot men. 39 of these had been committed nearby, in Cornbury. Here they had taken 13 oaks, 10 hazels, 6 thorns, 9 'loads of vert', and one maple. The freemen of Walcot had only small landholdings, and presumably they could only keep going by making use of the Forest.

Punishments, however, were lighter than before, normally a fine of half a mark (in an age when men could be hanged for theft), and mercy was often shown. In 1229 the King 'remits from Geoffrey Gothirde, John the son of Matilda, and Gilbert Dod, his anger and indignation on account of fawnskins taken with them in the Forest of Wychwood, and orders Thomas de Langley to set them free;' and in 1232 Walter de Blokesham, Robert de Dichele, William de Radford, William de Combe, and others, who were found with venison in the forest, were also pardoned.

Foresters themselves were sometimes guilty of offences against Forest Law. In 1230 Thomas was suspended from his post for unspecified tres-passes, and also lost the four acres of land which King John had given him. However, he was only out of office for three months, and a fine of £100 settled the problem. He got his land back, and the following year was granted a further acre, called Notteridge, 'right before the door of the said Thomas', for the building of a chapel; maybe this was a penance, or a sign of the King's renewed favour. (The name survives in Notteridge Copse, quarter of a mile west of the present Langley Farm.) Henry III's frequent presence at Woodstock must have brought him into close contact with Thomas, and this may have helped him get off with a fine on this occasion. The Justice of the Forests had been reluctant to lift Thomas's suspension and the King had to write a second time to insist on it.

In 1251 William de Langley was fined 30 marks for not keeping his bailiwick in good enough condition for the King's hunting, and at an Inquisition of the Forest made in the final year of Henry III's reign, 1272, William's son (possibly grandson), another Thomas, was in rather deeper trouble. The Verderers were escorting the visiting Justice of the Forest, Henry de Burghull, and seem to have deliberately guided him past Cornbury, which he found 'wasted of old and again newly, not only as regards oaks on the ground, but as regards outer branches of trees and underwood, through bad keeping of the foresters under the said Thomas.' Presumably the men of Walcot had been active, and Thomas had not reported it. The Justice also 'found the wood of Cornbury wholly devoured by beasts and torn up by hogs.' A spirit of live and let live was to everyone's advantage, and one wonders what Thomas had done to offend the Verderers. It seems that the de Langleys ruled Wychwood with a fairly light hand, for there are none of the complaints against the Forester's oppression that are common in other Royal Forests. This may have been because they were under the eye of the King at Woodstock; but it may also result from the hereditary nature of their office. They were local landowners, not royal officials imposed from outside, and had an interest in keeping on good terms with their neighbours.

Since the Forest boundaries were continually in dispute, and it was not always clear who had rights to what, the Forester had to tread carefully. In 1232 Thomas was ordered to allow the men of Stonesfield, Combe and Hanborough to pasture their goats in Wychwood 'as they used to have them in the time of King John, until the King directs otherwise; and he is to release the goats of those men, which he took and still keeps.' By now these were royal manors, and the King looked after his own. In 1290 there was trouble when the Bishop of Winchester, who had a chase within the Forest near Witney, was accused of killing deer and assarting waste land. The Sheriff of Oxford was ordered not to interfere with him or his followers, as he had a charter from the King, which 'those who held the inquest were ignorant of.'

The fourteenth century sees first the rise of the de Langley family to some eminence, and then their disappearance from the scene altogether.

When the first Thomas died c.1240 he was succeeded by his brother William. After him there may well be a generation missing from the records, as the next Lord of the Manor of Langley, and Forester of Wychwood, Thomas, was still under age in 1260. He died in 1280, and was succeeded by his son John, who was also under age. His tenure would be a troubled one. In 1317 he was summoned to the King's army at Newcastle-on-Tyne, to serve both in the war against the Scots, and against English rebels under the Earl of Lancaster. Edward II's campaign against Robert Bruce was a failure, and it may be that John was captured by the Scots and had to be ransomed; and he also became involved in opposition to Edward, for which he was twice pardoned in 1323. The consequent financial difficulties forced him, in effect, to mortgage his estate and the bailiwick of Wychwood to one Thomas West. John died in 1324; the custody of the Forest was returned to his son four years later, though repaying the debt to West took longer.

This son, Thomas, was the first de Langley to be knighted, and he became a leading figure in the county. He was chosen as a Knight of the Shire five times between 1335 and 1360, he was a collector in Oxfordshire of subsidies granted by parliament to the King, and sat on many commissions of *oyer et terminer*, which were appointed to enquire into serious crimes. In modern terms he was a tax collector and magistrate.

A variety of other important duties came his way. In 1330 he was given the custody of the Abbey of Bruern, which 'for want of good rule had fallen into decay and debt.' Together with Abbot Roger, he arranged a loan of one hundred pounds from two citizens of London, which was repaid in silver four years later. However, the financial management of Bruern did not improve, and in 1351 Thomas was called on again to sort out its affairs, together with other local notables, Edmund de Bereford (Barford), William de Shareshull, and John Golafre of Sarsden. This time they took over the running of the Abbey estate altogether, allowing the monks no more than was needed for food and clothing.

In 1349, he was appointed, this time with William de Shareshull and Richard de Williamscote, to investigate the complaint of the people of Finstock and Tapwell (a vanished hamlet on the site of the present Topples Wood) that they had been unfairly taxed compared with the people of Charlbury. This was in the immediate aftermath of the Black Death, which had reduced the population of the country by a third, when tax-gathering must have been exceptionally difficult. Legally, Finstock, Tapwell and Fawler were all hamlets of the market town of Charlbury.

They found that the complainants had indeed been assessed 'improvidently', and 'by the malice of the assessors and collectors.' As a result 'the men of Finstock and Tapwell are reduced to such misery and want by these assessments that some having abandoned their houses are compelled to seek their food by their own bodily labours, after abandoning their houses, and others beg from door to door.' Sir Thomas and his colleagues made a new assessment, whereby the tax for Finstock and Tapwell was reduced from £4. 11s. 8d. to £1. 18s. 3d., while that for Charlbury was raised from £3. 4s. 6d. to £5. 15s. 9d. Sir Thomas's other duties included the enforcement of the Statute of Labourers after the Black Death, and membership of a Commission 'to survey all gorces, mills, stanks, stakes and kiddles in the water of the Thames between London and Oxford, constructed in the time of Edward I and down to the present time, and to cause such as obstruct the passage to be removed.'

At the same time Sir Thomas had been making good use of the Forest for his own advantage, and after his death, in 1362, this was revealed by a *post mortem* inquisition. Three years before, he had cut down forty young oaks to make a paling round his garden; he had built houses in his manor of Langley, where houses had never been, 'by colour of his bailiwick'; he had built a grange, partly with the King's timber, and upon the King's land, and had occupied it for ten years without paying anything for it; he had built a grange and tan-yard in his manor of Milton, the same in his manor of Shorthampton, and a mill called Langley Mill, which was not in his manor of Langley, but in the demesne of Shipton, for all of which he had used the King's timber. He had also cut down fifty oaks at Notteridge; and 'made a pit to take clay in the ground of the King to his own use, and to the damage of the Lord the King.' This account reveals, in some detail, what had no doubt been the common practice of his ancestors down the centuries.

A few years before, Sir Thomas had made legal arrangements to ensure that Langley Manor and the bailiwick of Wychwood would be inherited by his sons; but 1361 saw the reappearance of the Black Death in England, which within a year carried off all the male members of the family. With them the name of de Langley died out. Sir Thomas's estate was divided among his sisters' descendants, but within a few years they had disposed of their rights in the Forest to Roger de Elmerugge, who had been Keeper of the Park at Woodstock. The de Langleys claimed to have held the bailiwick of the Forest since the Conquest, that is, for three centuries; Wychwood would never experience again such continuity of guardianship.

♣ 3

Cornbury Park

Apart from the annual payment into the Exchequer, Cornbury almost disappears from the historical record after the days of Henry I. However in 1312, in the Exchequer Accounts, it is referred to for the first time as a 'park'. When a park was created, it ceased to be subject to Forest Law, and any common rights of pasture there were lost. It had to be enclosed by a wall, or fence and ditch, which made hunting easier, since the wall prevented the deer escaping. The requirement to wall or fence a park meant that its boundaries were usually more or less circular, for reasons of cost, so we cannot be sure how close the boundaries of Cornbury Park are to those of the preceding Forest of Cornbury.

Cornbury may have been turned into a park to make hunting easier; but we also know it was used as a royal stud-farm. There are entries in the accounts for grooms, and for the provision of hay for the stallions. In the 1337 Close Rolls we find the first reference to a building at Cornbury, a lodge of stone and timber: the Exchequer is ordered to pay for this, also for 'a stone wall about the park, a dike of wood forty feet broad by the circuit of the park near the paling thereof, and other dikes by the middle of the park, and two deer leaps in that park.' A deer leap was a fence or wall with one side higher than the other, so that deer could leap over it in one direction only, into the park. The name of Buckleap Copse in the Forest probably records the site of one of them, as does Sore Leap near Waterman's Lodge. (A sore was a buck in its fourth year.)

In 1317 Roger de la Chaumbre was appointed Keeper of Cornbury, and its custody was taken away from the de Langleys. Both John and, later, Thomas de Langley petitioned for its return on the grounds that it was a heritage from their ancestors, but to no avail; and for much of the next three centuries Cornbury and Wychwood were under separate management.

Hugh Clifford is recorded as Keeper in 1328 and 1331; John de Solers was 'Keeper of the King's mares at Cornbury' in 1339, and John Squyer, King's yeoman, was appointed Keeper for life in 1349.

After the death of Sir Thomas de Langley in 1361 there was little continuity of guardianship over the Forest, and the same is true of Cornbury. To start with, both were in the care of local gentry or royal officials, whose names mean little; but gradually the offices came to be held by persons of some distinction. They must have been seen as increasingly profitable, and thus a suitable medium of patronage for the monarchs of the time.

In 1378 Cornbury was granted to 'the King's servitor' William Pepyr, 'during good behaviour, if no one else had an estate therein for life by grant of the late king'. In 1381 he was instructed to enclose the Park with a hedge and a ditch; and in 1383 Philip Rose and William Riche were appointed to take stonemasons and other labourers to build a wall around it. Maybe the wall ordered in 1337 had decayed, or never been built.

Pepyr's exact status is not altogether clear, since some accounts were rendered in 1381 by a Sir Philip de la Vache, who is described as farmer and keeper of the King's manors of Woodstock and Hanborough, and of the King's parks at Woodstock and Cornbury. These accounts are interesting, in that they show us something of the expense of maintaining the parks and the deer. The annual provision of hay for the deer in Woodstock and Cornbury, including the transport and stacking, cost £38. 5s. 11d. Brushwood, 'for the support of the King's deer', came to £2. 6s. The cost of stakes for repairing the hedges, at 1d per cartload, was 2s. 4d., and the labour costs (4 men at 3d per day each) were 28s. Apart from this the total wage bill came to £39. 5s. 8d. The Keeper's deputy, who was responsible for both parks, was paid 100s. per year; two chaplains, employed to pray for the souls of the King's ancestors at Woodstock, were paid the same. The 'parkers', two at Woodstock and one at Cornbury, got 3d. per day each, 'one gatekeeper and one gardener' 2d., and the overseer of the King's work and of the workmen, 1½d.

Maybe Pepyr was Sir Philip's deputy; or even the 'parker' of Cornbury – if the latter, then he was paid no more than the labourers repairing the hedges. But this seems unlikely, since when he retired from the custody of Cornbury in 1402 he was replaced by a man unquestionably of high rank – Sir William Willecotes, of Wilcote, who had been a Member of

Parliament and Sheriff. In 1409 the right to the Keepership was extended from Sir William's lifetime to that of his heirs. He died in 1411, and is buried with his wife in the Wilcote Chapel of North Leigh Church.

His heirs presumably held Cornbury until 1437, when it passed to an even more distinguished figure, Richard Beauchamp, Earl of Warwick. He had local connections, as his family had owned land in the area, including the manor of Spelsbury, since the thirteenth century. An inquisition in 1446, seven years after his death, shows that he held, among much else, the manors of Burford and Langley, and land in Milton, Shipton, Ascott, Shorthampton, Walcot and Leafield. Warwick had travelled widely, had visited the Holy Sepulchre in Jerusalem, and was known throughout Europe as a brave and chivalrous warrior; the dying Henry V had entrusted to him the education of his infant son Henry VI. In the same year that he was granted Cornbury he was relieved by the Council of responsibility for the young King, and was appointed Lieutenant of France and Normandy. He remained there until his death in Rouen in 1439, so it is unlikely that Cornbury ever saw him.

The terms of the grant in 1437 spell out in detail the humble origins of its value: Warwick's rights included 'all dead wood, old hedges, pannage, fern, heath, windfalls, and whatsoever is thrown down to feed the deer and by the wind, water, fisheries, meadows, feedings, and pastures in the said park, top-wood and the bark of fallen trees in the park, saving always hay and pasture sufficient for the King's deer.'

Within a few months of Warwick's death Cornbury passed to William de la Pole, 4th Earl and later Duke of Suffolk, and his wife Alice, the granddaughter of Geoffrey Chaucer; though the day after the initial grant another grant was made in the same terms, adding the name of John Golofre to those of Suffolk and his wife. The Golofres, who had held Sarsden since the Conquest, and were related to the de Langleys, had held many Forest offices over the centuries, and John Golafre may well have taken day-to-day care of the Park. Suffolk, like Warwick, was a major political figure, whose family estate was at Ewelme. As commander of the English army in France he had been defeated and captured by Joan of Arc. Later, in 1450, he became the victim of popular anger at the loss of English lands in France, was banished, and murdered at sea. Like others connected with Cornbury during these years, Suffolk is a familiar figure to readers of Shakespeare's History Plays.

On reaching maturity Henry VI had granted Wychwood to a childhood friend, Lord Sudeley, in terms whose generosity would form the basis of legal disputes as late as the nineteenth century, and it seems that Cornbury was included. However, given the prolonged conflict between York and Lancaster, no grant was secure, and when Edward IV seized the throne in 1461 he gave the Keepership of Cornbury to Richard Harcourt of Stanton Harcourt. Later Sir Richard, he became Sheriff of Oxfordshire and M.P., and held the county in the interest of Edward IV at the time of the latter's rupture with Warwick the Kingmaker in 1468. He inherited Wytham Manor from his elder brother and built the present Manor House there. He may also have been responsible for some building at Cornbury, since his coat of arms, and those of his three wives, were recorded when Richard Lee, Portcullis Pursuivant at the College of Arms, made a Herald's Visitation of Cornbury in 1574.

Sir Richard, as a noted Yorkist, could not keep his offices after Bosworth, and in 1486 the Keepership of Cornbury was given to Anthony Fettiplace. Descendants of one of the ushers of William the Conqueror, the Fettiplaces were a family of great local importance, owning land in fifteen counties. Their memory, together with that of the Traceys of Stanway and the Lacys of Shipton-under-Wychwood, is preserved in the rhyme:

The Traceys, the Lacys, and the Fettiplaces,
Own all the manors, the parks and the chases.

Earlier in the century they had moved from Berkshire to Swinbrook, where Anthony built a manor house in 1490, and where his memorial brass was placed in the church on his death in 1510. At the 1574 Heralds' Visitation his coat of arms was also noted on a bedstead at Cornbury. His main importance in the story of Cornbury, however, lies in the fact that the oldest part of the present house, the North-west, or Tudor Wing, may have been built about 1495, and thus during his tenure. A three-storied gabled building, with a single-story extension at the northern end, it has stone-mullioned windows and lead-glazed casements, some of which were filled in or replaced in the seventeenth century. If any remnants of an earlier building survive, they have been completely absorbed in its replacement.

Anthony Fettiplace died in 1510, shortly after Henry VIII succeeded to the throne. Henry, even more clearly than his predecessors, used the lands of Wychwood and Cornbury as rewards for his friends, and in 1511 William

Compton became both Keeper of Cornbury and Ranger of Wychwood. A few years older than Henry, William Compton had become his page at the age of eleven, and chief gentleman of the bedchamber on Henry's accession. He accompanied Henry to the Field of the Cloth of Gold in1520, and was awarded many honours, including the Chancellorship of Ireland, and the right to wear his hat in the King's presence. It is unlikely that he had much time for Wychwood and Cornbury; his main private interest was in rebuilding and emparking his ancestral estate at Compton Wynyates in Warwickshire. He died of the sweating sickness in 1528, whereupon his offices were granted to Henry Norris, another friend of Henry's youth, but also a man with local connections. At that time he was not only close to the King, but also to Anne Boleyn, the future Queen. Eventually he seems to have become too close to her, was implicated in her fall, and executed on Tower Hill in 1536, two days before Anne herself.

Norris had joint successors in two brothers from a Gloucestershire family, Sir John and Sir Thomas Brydges, who were granted the offices later in 1536, 'in survivorship' – i.e. if one died, the other retained the offices. Not only did they hold Cornbury and Wychwood, but also the manors of Minster Lovell, Burford, Shipton, Spelsbury and Langley, and the bailiwick of Chadlington. Sir John spent many years in France, campaigning or peacemaking, as politics dictated. In 1553 he was summoned to the support of Lady Jane Grey but 'much addicted to the old religion' gave his allegiance to Mary. As a reward he was appointed Lieutenant of the Tower of London, and in this capacity accompanied Lady Jane Grey to the scaffold, and had the custody of Princess Elizabeth. He played a large part in the suppression of Sir Thomas Wyatt's rebellion, and superintended the burning of Bishop Hooper in Gloucester in 1555. Before his death in 1556 he had been created Lord Chandos of Sudeley.

His younger brother Thomas was much more closely connected with Oxfordshire. He was probably resident at Cornbury for much of the time, where he was responsible for the management of both the Park and the Forest. The likelihood is that Sir John, having acquired the offices in their joint names, handed them over to his brother. Sir Thomas plotted a skilful course through the lethal politics of the time. Under Henry VIII he held many offices in the county, and acquired the old monastic lands at Bruern. Under Edward he was active in stripping churches of their

A lake at Cornbury.

decorations, and selling off chantry lands. Yet in Mary's reign he was Sheriff of Oxfordshire, in which capacity he attended the burning of Archbishop Cranmer. Then in 1558 he was elected M.P. for Oxfordshire in Elizabeth's first Parliament. It is hardly surprising that his personal religious loyalties remain unknown.

For a short period during the Brydges' custody of Cornbury, it passed into the ownership of John Dudley, Earl of Warwick (later Duke of Northumberland). In January 1550 he exchanged various estates with Edward VI, receiving among much else both Cornbury and Wychwood. In December of the following year he sold them back to the King, so that Cornbury's time under his ownership was brief, but it may have been at this time that the Tudor Wing was built, if indeed it had not been built in the 1490s. Architectural historians have come to no conclusion, and judging by its style it could have been built at either date.

We do know, however, that during his tenure Sir Thomas created three fishponds and stocked them with carp, eels, and bream. The largest pool measured 12 score yards by fourscore, the others were eight score and four score yards square respectively. Though their dimensions are different, these are presumably the forerunners of the present ponds at Cornbury: the ponds in the valley of Newell Brook have changed their number and size several times over the centuries.

Sir Thomas's will, dated from Cornbury a month before his death in 1559, shows that he was a benefactor to the parishes of Charlbury, Burford, Shipton, Swinbrook, Spelsbury and Swerford; and he and his wife were both buried in Charlbury Church. The inscription on the memorial brass to his wife Joan, who had died in 1541, was recorded by Antony à Wood in the seventeenth century. The brass itself had been stolen long before the twentieth century, but its stone frame, decorated with the arms of Brydges and his wife, survived on the south wall of the Pudlicote aisle, and in 1905 a replica brass plate was placed within it by Vernon Watney. The inscription, if correctly transcribed by à Wood, is historically interesting, as it refers to Henry VIII as 'on earth Supreme Head of the Church of England and Ireland'.

Brydges' successor as Keeper of Cornbury, though not of Wychwood, was John Fortescue of Shirburn in Oxfordshire. When he was only six, in 1539, his father, Sir Adrian Fortescue, had been executed for his loyalty to Rome (and was beatified by the Pope in 1885). His mother, however, had taken as her second husband Thomas Parry, who was the Princess Elizabeth's most loyal follower during her imprisonment under Mary. Fortescue makes his first appearance in history in 1555, during Elizabeth's imprisonment at Woodstock, when he was caught by her gaoler trying to smuggle some books and letters to her. He probably joined her household soon after; he was also her second cousin, through his Boleyn grandmother. His subsequent career shows the lasting trust she placed in him. On Elizabeth's accession he was appointed Keeper of the Great Wardrobe, retaining this post until the end of her reign 44 years later. He became M.P. for Wallingford in 1572, and later for Buckingham. He was later Chancellor of the Exchequer, and Chancellor of the Duchy of Lancaster. Not surprisingly he became very rich, and built a large mansion on his estate at Salden in Buckinghamshire. Towards the end of her life the Queen remarked that two men had outdone her expectation: 'Walsingham for subtlety and officious service, and Fortescue for integrity.'

Fortescue was not normally resident at Cornbury, as Sir Thomas Brydges had been, and there are various shreds of evidence about possible tenants of the house at this time. In 1574, as we have seen above, there was a Heralds' Visitation when many coats of arms of previous tenants were

Sir John Fortescue.

recorded; the house is referred to here as 'Mr. Stafford's house at Cornbury Park'. This is almost certainly Thomas Stafford, son of William Stafford of Tattenhoe in Buckinghamshire, near Fortescue's estate at Salden. Stafford had strong links with Cornbury, being related through his mother to the Fettiplaces, the Brydges, and the Fortescues. A 'Thomas Stafford Gent.' is mentioned in the Rolls of Lay Subsidies (a form of taxation) under

Charlbury in 1566, and under Cornbury in 1576. Four of his children were baptised in Charlbury Church between 1565 and 1575, which suggests he was continuously resident during that time. In 1577 on the death of his stepfather he seems to have left Cornbury for Tattenhoe, where he was buried 30 years later.

But he is not the only person recorded as resident at Cornbury during these years. The chronicler Holinshed writes that an Irish peer, Lord Trimelston, sickened and died in 1572, while staying in the house of a 'worshipful matron' called Margaret Tiler at Cornbury. Three years later another Irish peer, Lord Dunsany, was living at Cornbury when he was questioned on behalf of the Star Chamber about a possible Catholic conspiracy against the Queen. Dunsany, who had a reputation for great learning, and was a grandmaster of the Guild of the Virgin Mary of Killeen, was cleared of any suspicion, and was soon asking the Queen to relieve 'his poor condition'. This may point to a series of temporary tenancies, which were probably also common in those numerous earlier periods when there was no resident Keeper. However, there is a connection between Lord Trimelston, whose family name was Barnewell, and Lord Dunsany, who had married the daughter of his guardian, also called Barnewell; but how Thomas Stafford and Margaret Tiler fit into the picture, if at all, remains a mystery.

Another name associated with Cornbury during the reign of Elizabeth is that of Robert Dudley, Earl of Leicester. The favourite of the Queen for many years, he was one of the most powerful figures of the age, but his connection with Cornbury is much slighter than legend has asserted. For several years during the 1580s he held Langley and Wychwood, but there is no record of any grant to him of Cornbury. However, a number of his letters are dated from there, and he may well have reached a friendly agreement with Fortescue to use the house when he was in the area. There is, however, no evidence that Queen Elizabeth ever stayed there: her only recorded visit was one of a mere few hours in 1572.

Leicester may not have had much to do with Cornbury during his life, except as an occasional resident, but it was there that he died, on September 4th 1588. This, however, was somewhat fortuitous: he had been travelling from London to his main estate at Kenilworth when he had fallen ill of a fever and took refuge at Cornbury. His body was taken to the Beauchamp Chapel in Warwick to be buried. A room at the south end of

Robert Dudley, Earl of Leicester.

the Tudor Wing at Cornbury in which, according to tradition, he died, was later named after him.

After Leicester's death his Rangership of Wychwood was granted to Fortescue, and Wychwood and Cornbury were now finally reunited under the same management, as they have remained ever since. When

Part of the Tudor wing with the Leicester Room on the upper floor; and the west end of the Danby wing.

the Queen died in 1603 Fortescue's position might have seemed in danger, as he had opposed James I's succession, but the new king appreciated his qualities, and kept him on as Chancellor of the Duchy, and Master of the Great Wardrobe. In 1603 he entertained James at Salden, and in 1605 at Cornbury, where despite a lavish entertainment he suffered, as many did, from James's drunken rudeness: 'he at his parting laughed, and made unseemly gesture in the porch.' Sir John Fortescue died in 1607, and the custody of Wychwood and Cornbury then passed to his son Sir Francis.

In 1606 the Park was enlarged by enclosing some meadows to the south of the Newell stream; this became known as the Little Park. A grant of £220 was made by the Exchequer for building new walls, and a further £25 was granted in 1611 to finish the work. The invoice tells us something about the expense of walling:

	£.	s.	d.
John Launsbury and other labourers for digging of stones for the building of the said walls viz: for every pearche two loades after the rate of 2½d the lode amounting to the sum of	57	0	7
Thomas Thorne, mason, and divers other masons for making of 265 pearches of wall in length being seven foot in height, on the east syde of the said parke to inclose the said meadows, after the rate of 3.2d the pearche, amounting to the some of	57	15	10
Peter Fletcher carpenter for making of two gates for the said walls and for ironwork for the same 60/-, and for making of one bridge within the said parke and repairing of the old bridges there 40/- in all		100/-	
Carriage of the said 5,475 lodes of stones from the places where the same was digged unto the place where the said wall was built, after the rate of 5½d for every lode, amount to the sum of	125	9	4½

In 1610 a Special Committee of the Exchequer was appointed to find out how many mills the King owned in Cornbury, and an enquiry was held in Charlbury on June 6th. They found that in Elizabeth's reign there had been one watermill, on the site of the present Southill, and that 'the millers thereof had all the pools, ponds and waters coming out of the forest of Wychwood, called Newell Brook'. Eight years before, however, the old mill had been pulled down, and three mills built in the same place under one roof; there were three millponds totalling about four acres, but at some times of the year the water from Newell Brook was barely sufficient to drive a single mill. The whole premises were worth 6s. 8d. per year.

Not long after inheriting the custody of Cornbury and Wychwood from his father, Francis Fortescue found himself with a new overlord. In October 1610 James I gave both to his sixteen year old son Henry, Prince of Wales, 'for the augmentation of the Duchy of Cornwall'. Henry, however, died two years later, and in 1617 Cornbury and Wychwood were granted to his younger brother Charles, who had become Prince of Wales the previous year. A committee of courtiers, including Sir Francis Bacon, was instructed to 'hold Wychwood and Cornbury for ninety-nine years to the behoof of the said Prince of Wales.'

By then, however, Fortescue was no longer Keeper; in 1615 the Keepership of Cornbury and the Rangership of Wychwood passed to Henry Lord Danvers, his heirs and assigns, 'so long as any male heir of Sir John Fortescue survived'. This proviso suggests that Fortescue had sold his interest in Cornbury and Wychwood to Danvers; his main estate, after all, was at Salden. Danvers, however, was to make his home at Cornbury, and his arrival marks a new and important stage in its history.

4

The Earl of Danby

Henry Danvers, who became Baron Danvers in 1603, and Earl of Danby in 1626, had a long and successful military career, and held many important public offices, yet also enjoyed a reputation as a scholar and patron of learning. John Aubrey, who was a distant relation, wrote of him: 'He perfected his Latin when a man by parson Oldham of Dodmerton; was a perfect master of the French; a historian; tall and spare; temperate; sedate and solid; a very great favourite of Prince Henry... All his servants were sober and wise in their respective places.'

He was born in 1573 at Dauntsey in Wiltshire, where the Danvers had lived for generations. One of his remote ancestors was William de Langley, the Forester of Wychwood who died in 1259. According to Aubrey his father, Sir John, was 'a most beautiful and good and even-tempered person.' His mother, however, sounds more formidable: 'an Italian, prodigious parts for a Woman. I have heard my father's mother say that she had Chaucer at her fingers' ends. A great politician; great witt and spirit, but revengefull. Knew how to manage her estate as well as any man; understood jewells as well as any jeweller.'

The young Henry became a page to Sir Philip Sidney, and was probably present when Sidney died after the Battle of Zutphen in 1586. He continued in military service in France and the Low Countries, and was knighted by the Earl of Essex in 1591 at the siege of Rouen. However, in 1594 he and his elder brother Charles killed a Wiltshire neighbour in the course of a local feud, and had to flee the country. While in exile, they served in the French army and won the approval of Henri IV, who asked Queen Elizabeth to pardon them. At the same time they were gaining credit at home by acting as secret agents on behalf of Sir Robert Cecil and the Earl of Essex. In 1597 Henry returned to the English service and commanded

Henry Danvers, Earl of Danby. (From a portrait by Vandyke.)

a man-of-war under the Earl of Nottingham, who called him 'one of the best captains in the fleet.' In the following year he and his brother received their pardon, and on their return home after 4 years' exile the church bells in Dauntsey and the surrounding villages were rung in triumphant celebration. According to Aubrey, this was his mother's doing: 'To obtain pardons for her sonnes she maryed Sir Edmund Carey, cosen-german to Queen Elizabeth, but kept him to hard meate.'

By 1599 Henry was away again, fighting in Ireland. There he remained for several years, firstly as Lieutenant-General of the Horse, later as Governor of Armagh, and Sergeant-Major-General of the Army. His career does not seem to have been affected by his brother Charles's execution in 1601 for his involvement in Essex's rebellion. During his time in Ireland he was shot in the face, and received the wound which is visible in portraits of him by Vandyke and others.

Under James I his career continued to flourish, and in July 1603 he was created Baron Danvers for his 'valiant service at Kinsale'. In 1607 he was appointed Lord President of Munster, a post which he kept until 1615, when he sold it to the Earl of Thomond for £3200. It was in the same year that he took over Wychwood and Cornbury from Sir Francis Fortescue, and it was at Cornbury that he spent much of the rest of his life. His health was declining, and he became increasingly reluctant to leave the peace of the Oxfordshire countryside for public duties.

In 1621 he was appointed Governor of Guernsey for life, but he rarely went there. The Privy Council were displeased, and in 1627 he wrote to them in some anger ('much animated' by their letter) that he was being required to secure the safety of the Channel Islands, without sufficient supplies or men being provided, and that the Council could hardly expect him to go there if he had not the means to defend them. After many delays, in March 1629 he did actually reach Jersey, but by April he was back in England, forced to return by lack of victuals, and money with which to pay the garrison. He was then immediately ordered to France, probably in connection with the attempt to relieve La Rochelle, but wrote to the Earl of Carlisle pleading ill-health: 'He was forced to take leave of absence for a few days. On precedent experience he found nothing saved his life but the quiet of Cornbury Lodge, and the counsel of his old physician Dr Ashworth, who knows every vein amiss in his body.' Later, in July, his health forced him to 'suspend all his engagements'.

In 1633 he was made Knight of the Garter, and Aubrey contrasts the plainness of his manner with the flamboyance of the Scottish Earl of Morton, who was installed at the same time. 'The Scotish Earle (like Zeuxis his picture) adorned with all art and costlinesse: whilst our English Earle (like to the plain sheet of Apelles) by the gravity of habit, gott the advantage of the Gallantry of his Corrival with judicious beholders.' His plainness of dress was not due to poverty, however; Aubrey also tells us that he was 'a great Improver of his Estate, to eleaven thousand per annum at least, neer twelve. A great Oeconomist; He allowed three thousand pounds per annum only for his Kitchin.' This suggests hospitality on a magnificent scale. He also educated and advanced the careers of several young men, future Cavalier commanders during the Civil War. The most notable were the Legge brothers, William, Governor of Oxford in 1645, Richard and John, both Colonels in the royalist cavalry. The latter would both be Deputy Rangers of Wychwood after the Restoration.

Danby's wealth was not only spent on hospitality, but on improving and rebuilding Cornbury. Although only the 'Keeper' and not the owner, he must have felt secure enough in his possession to do so. In 1631 he instructed Nicholas Stone to build a new south-western wing, since known as the Danby wing. Stone is better known as a sculptor, but he had worked for seven years under Hendrik de Keyser, master-mason to the City of Amsterdam, and had later been Inigo Jones's Master-Mason at the Banqueting House in Whitehall. He had also worked at Holyrood and St. James' Palace, and on the portico of Old St. Paul's Cathedral; and would later build the porch of the University Church in Oxford. In his account book for 1631 Stone wrote that he had visited Cornbury 33 times over two years, and that his fee was £1000. Cornbury is the only house that Stone designed, and is one of the very first examples in England of the classical style used for a private house. The contractor for the building was Timothy Strong of Barrington, whose grandsons later worked for Wren at St. Paul's.

The eastern half of the new wing was taken up by the Stone Hall, while the western end contained a Buttery with bedrooms above. Between the two a porch opened on to what was later a lawn. Beneath, a range of stone-vaulted cellars ran the whole length of the wing. The Stone Hall is named either after its builder or after its stone floor, of which the antiquary Robert Plot wrote in 1677: 'At Cornbury Park there was a sort of Stone, the Quarry

Above: The south-west, or Danby, wing.
Below: The porch in the Danby wing.

whereof is now quite exhausted, that never would sweat in the moistest Weather, of which the Pavement of the Hall in the House there still remains as a sufficient Testimony.' About 30 years later the wing was considerably altered, and an upper floor added at the east end, but the Hall was origi-nally the full height of the building, with a ceiling consisting of a flat, three-centred arch, divided into panels by large mouldings, and with a cartouche at each end. There was a traditional oak screen at one end, to protect the porch entrance, and the sites of the oak posts were still in 1910 clearly defined on the old stone floor. From outside, the central porch remains as Stone built it, and a small door and oval window at the west corner; the architraves and keystones of the ground floor windows are also probably his work.

During work carried out at the beginning of the twentieth century an old well dating from this time was discovered in a courtyard near the Hall. Six feet in diameter, it is lined with the same stone that was used for the House, and contains a winding stone staircase of about 120 steps with two niches as passing places. It leads to a stream of running water at the bottom.

The style of the building may have been quite new, but the scale and height of the Hall, reminiscent of the slightly earlier Hall at Chastleton House a few miles away, which still survives, shows that the way of life Danby followed at Cornbury was a traditional one. Here he extended his generous hospitality, kept his large household, and brought up young men as his pages, as he had been brought up in the household of Sir Philip Sidney.

At the same time Danby employed Stone at the Botanical Garden in Oxford. Danby had studied at Christ Church, and wanted to give the University 'a place whereby learning, especially the faculty of medicine, might be improved.' In 1621 he bought five acres opposite Magdalen College, formerly a Jewish cemetery, raised and enclosed it. It was long thought that the main gate, built ten years later, was designed by Inigo Jones, but Pevsner attributes it to Stone, and the work formed part of the same contract by which he built Cornbury. The gate is inscribed:

GLORIAE DEI OPT. MAX. HONORI CAROLI REGIS, IN USUM
ACAD. ET REIPUB. HENRICUS COMES DANBY
DD.MDCXXXII.

In a niche in the main pediment there is a bust of Danby, by John Vanderstein, placed there in 1695. During his life Danby spent £5000 on the Garden, and left an income from his Parsonage of Kirkdale in Yorkshire, to maintain it, and to cover the salaries of a Professor and a gardener.

Even when he was at Cornbury Danby was not left free to enjoy his retirement. In 1631 he was appointed to a special commission to enquire into the operation of the Poor Law, payment of relief for soldiers and mariners, maintenance of houses of correction, punishment of rogues and vagabonds, repressing drunkenness, etc., etc. In the same year the King ordered him to build a new wall around the whole of Wychwood 'for the preservation of His Majesty's game.' And then Charles discovered the 'Enstone Marvels', a complex of fountains, springs and grottoes created by Thomas Bushell. Bushell, who has been described as 'a speculative and generally unsuccessful engineer', was an eccentric figure who had spent three years as a hermit on the Isle of Lundy. Aubrey wrote of him that 'he had the strangest bewitching to drawe-in people (yea, discreet and wary men) into his projects that ever I heard of.'

He certainly had this effect on the King, who should surely have had more important things on his mind. Another visitor had found the Marvels 'a mad gimcrack', but the King and Queen were fascinated by them. Perhaps unfortunately for himself, Danby was conveniently placed to see that the King's wishes were carried out. In 1635 the King wrote to him:

> According to His Majesty's former directions, the Earl's care has been to preserve that rarity of nature near Enstone, which was first discovered by Thomas Bushell, and brought to maturity through his industrious charge. His Majesty, having viewed the place of that natural curiosity, not only thinks fit that the rock ought to be preserved, but ornated with groves, walks, fishponds, gardens and waterworks, and to that end he has taken the said rock into his protection, and given directions to Bushell for perfecting so good a work. For better enabling Bushell's endeavours, the King desires the Earl to call such as it may concern for disposing the highway to some other place, which may be most convenient to His Majesty's design, trusting he will find no man so refractory as he should have cause to certify his obstinacy to the King.

The inhabitants of Enstone, however, did prove obstinate and refractory. They disliked their highway being diverted to please the King's whim, and in 1637 the Council had to instruct the local Justices:

> Hearing that some of the copyholders of the manor out of a malignant disposition had fined Bushell for having turned the said

highway, and some having cut down trees planted for beautifying the said rock, and others having presumed to forbid his workmen employed in setting up a wall for preserving the groves and the walks...the justices are not only to see that the work is done by the time His Majesty shall come to Wood Grove, but also...to deliver such as are delinquent to the custody of Edmund Barker...

Whether Danby played any part in this we do not know: maybe he pleaded age and ill-health.

Though a Royalist, Danby was far from approving all the King's actions, and in 1636 he had formally protested to Charles about the imposition of ship money, and urged him to recall Parliament. It may have been to secure his support at the outbreak of the Civil War that in 1642 the King confirmed Danby in his offices in Wychwood Forest, and gave him Cornbury Park 'for ever'. This included 'all houses, underwoods, trees, etc., the enclosing wall, etc., with the meadow called Littleham, in the parish of Charlbury, next to the walls of the park, containing two roods.' Danby surrendered the fees he had received as Keeper, but was still liable to pay £20 per annum rent to the King, so the Crown must have retained the freehold. Danby, one suspects, did not need this incentive to support Charles, and though age prevented him joining the royal army, he sent the King the sizeable sum of £3,400.

There is little evidence about what part Cornbury played, if any, in the war, but the remains of a gun battery of that time are to be found on rising ground above the Evenlode, about 600 yards to the east of Cornbury House. The earthworks, now partly surrounded by a small plantation, can still easily be seen. They consist of three sides of a rectangle, with earth banks 116 feet long. There is a six-foot gap in the southern bank, to be used as an embrasure for cannon, facing down the valley of the Evenlode, and covering the old road from Cornbury to Woodstock. It was probably constructed early in 1643, as part of the outlying defences of Charles's main base at Oxford (Woodstock and Bletchingdon were similarly fortified.) In 1644 a squadron of royal dragoons was based at Charlbury; but by 1646 Cornbury was certainly in Parliamentary hands, as the commander-in-chief, Thomas Fairfax, stayed there in October, together with General Ireton and his wife Bridget, Cromwell's daughter.

In January 1644 Danby died at Cornbury. He returned to his birthplace at Dauntsey for burial, and on his monument are lines attributed to the poet George Herbert, who was his brother's stepson. Modern scholars think the attribution unlikely, but if they are Herbert's they must have been written long before, since Herbert himself had died in 1633. The lines are in any case so unspecific, that they could have been written about anyone.

> Sacred Marble, safely keepe
> His dust who under thee must sleepe
> Until the graves againe restore
> Theire dead, and Time shalbe no more:
> Meane while, if hee (wch all thinges weares)
> Doe ruine thee; or if the teares
> Are shed for him, dissolve thy frame,
> Thou art requited; for his Fame,
> His Vertues, and his Worth shalbee
> Another Monument for Thee.

Danby never married, and in his will he takes care that Cornbury should not pass to his Parliamentarian younger brother, Sir John Danvers. Instead, he left it to his sister Katherine, Lady Gargrave, for her life, after which it was to pass to his nephew Henry Danvers, son of Sir John. His faithful servant and acting Ranger of Wychwood, Acton Drake, was granted a life interest in the manors of Great and Little Langley, the lease of King's Coppice, and Danby's bedroom furniture. Nor did Danby forget the Botanical Garden at Oxford. He had already provided an income from Kirkdale Parsonage for its support; and then in a codicil signed only a month before his death, he adds 'those C trees bought of my lord of Downes lying yet at Wilcote', for the completion of buildings at the Garden.

He had named William Lenthall of Burford, Speaker of the Commons, as an Overseer of his Will; then, in another codicil, he notes that since Lenthall felt his parliamentary duties might prevent him acting, he asks Sir Edward Hyde, Chancellor of the Exchequer, to take his place. He, perhaps tactfully, replaces a moderate Parliamentarian with a moderate Royalist. After the Restoration Hyde himself would become the owner of Cornbury.

Sir John Danvers, who had come out on the side of Parliament in 1642, was indignant at being left out of his brother's will, and persuaded the House of Commons in 1649 to pass a resolution that he had been unjustly excluded. This did not get him Cornbury, though, which had been declared State property. His son Henry had been granted the Rangership of Wychwood by Danby in 1643, when he was only 10 years old, but he died at the age of 21, in 1654, predeceasing his father, who then succeeded him. Sir John was a Member of Parliament for 35 years, and Clarendon, in his *History of the Rebellion*, writes of him that having been neglected by his brother, and contracted vast debts, 'being a proud, formal, weak man, between being seduced and a seducer,' he took it 'as a high honour to sit on the same bench with Cromwell, who employed and contemned him at once.' Thus he was recruited to the tribunal that sat in judgement on the King and was one of the signatories to Charles's death warrant. He was one of the only two judges who the King recognised.

Sir John's place in history is ensured not only by his being one of the Regicides, but by his enthusiasm for gardening, which was the cause of his massive debts. He was the first man to create Italian gardens in England – 'revolutionary', according to Roy Strong – first at his Chelsea home in the 1620s, and later on his Wiltshire estate at Lavington. The former contained sculptures by Nicholas Stone, who worked for Sir John before he worked for Danby. One cannot but feel that, had Sir John inherited Cornbury, and had the times been peaceful and funds sufficient, it would have become even more of a landmark in the history of English landed estates.

It is not clear whether Sir John or his sister, Lady Gargrave, spent any time at Cornbury or took an interest in it, and their involvement was complicated by the outcome of the Civil War. In July 1649 an Act was passed for the sale of the late King's possessions, but Cornbury Park was specifically excluded, and reserved for the use of the State. Danby had also been declared 'delinquent' for his adherence to the King, and the various beneficiaries of his will had to pay over £20,000 in composition. Lady Gargrave herself had to pay £5061 15s., which was handed over to her brother. In 1652 Cornbury was listed as one of 'divers castles' to be offered for sale, but appears not to have been sold, and Lady Gargrave was described on her death in 1660 as 'of Cornbury Park, co. Oxon.'

5

The Forest in Decline

Throughout the fifteenth and sixteenth centuries the day-to-day life of the Forest must have continued – the preservation and hunting of the deer, the cutting of timber, the clearing and re-enclosing of coppices, and the pasturing of animals. Verderers' courts were still held, and agistors and regarders appointed. The picture becomes confused as the royal government takes less interest and records become sparser, especially during the turmoil of the Wars of the Roses. The Forest remained a good source of profit for those who held its offices, but there was little significant change, and its history at this time, like that of Cornbury Park, is not much more than an incomplete list of names, mostly meaningless today, of those who held official responsibility for it.

From the later 14th Century Wychwood was sometimes 'granted' *in toto* to a member of the royal family, or leading nobleman. This meant the handing-over of all the royal privileges in the Forest, including the right to hunt. Henry VI's grant to Lord Sudeley allows him 'liberty to make reasonable and moderate hunting there for the solace of himself and his friends at proper times, and to take the wild beasts killed in hunting and to carry them away at pleasure, during his life; without disturbance from the King, his heirs, successors, justices, sheriffs, coroners, foresters, verderers, regarders, or other officers or ministers whatsoever, and without rendering anything therefor.' The grantee also received the fees paid by commoners for pasturing their cattle there, and the annual rental of £7 that normally went to the Exchequer.

The first such grantee was Anne of Bohemia, Richard II's Queen, who received on her marriage in 1381 estates throughout the country to a total value of £4,500, of which Wychwood formed only a small part. Queen Anne died in 1394, and in 1403 Henry IV granted the Forest to his second wife, Joan of Navarre. She kept it until her death in 1437, despite being imprisoned for several years during the reign of her stepson Henry V. In 1449 it was granted to Lord Sudeley, who died in 1473; no more such grants were made until the middle of the following century.

Under this regime there was still a Forester, usually one of the local gentry, or a royal official, but sometimes a person of higher rank. After the death of Sir Thomas de Langley in 1362 the Forest passed swiftly through several hands, and by 1378 it was held by Sir Thomas's son-in-law, Sir John Golofre of Sarsden. On Sir John's death in 1379 he was succeeded by his illegitimate son, also Sir John, whose illegitimacy was no bar to his achieving a high position at court and burial in Westminster Abbey on his death in 1396. His widow, Philippa, was swiftly married again, to Edward Plantagenet (the Aumerle of Shakespeare's *Richard II*), son of the Duke of York, who now held the Forest in right of his wife until 1405, when he was imprisoned on suspicion of plotting against Henry IV. He was pardoned, but lost his rights over Wychwood. In 1415 he was killed at the battle of Agincourt, one of the very few English casualties.

We can be sure that he did not carry out any of the day to day management of the Forest. This must have been done by deputies, often referred to as Rangers or Keepers, though eventually these titles become indistinguishable from that of Forester, and it can be hard to be sure about the holder's exact position in the Forest hierarchy. In 1398 William Coubrigge was appointed Ranger, and held the office until 1416, when he surrendered it to John Launce. In 1423, on the accession of Henry VI, he was confirmed in office, but was later replaced by William Halle. In 1432 Halle was succeeded by William Brian. But the following year he surrendered his post to no less a figure than Richard Beauchamp, 13th Earl of Warwick, who is unlikely to have held a merely subordinate position.

Wychwood remained with the Beauchamp family until 1446, when Henry VI's childhood friend Lord Sudeley became 'Master-Forester', a hitherto unknown title and presumably intended to emphasise his superior status. Three years later all the royal privileges in the Forest were granted to him, and Bernard de la Mare was appointed Keeper, soon succeeded by Richard Colstonfogge. Sudeley appears to have kept his privileges until his death in 1473, but whether he actually enjoyed them, given the political turbulence of the time, is less certain. In 1459 his stepson Lord Lovell (of

Minster Lovell) was appointed Chief Forester of Wychwood (another new title), but, as a Lancastrian, his tenure of this office may have been short; and Edward IV, shortly after his accession in 1461, granted the Rangership of Wychwood to 'his servant, Ralph Chiderowe of Calais, for life'.

In 1473 Wychwood returned to the Warwick family, in the person of Richard Beauchamp's granddaughter Isabel, who was married to the King's brother, George Duke of Clarence. Clarence was murdered in 1478, and the heir to his lands and titles was his infant son Edward Plantagenet. The last male Plantagenet, and with a strong claim to the throne of England, he spent most of his life in prison, until he was executed by Henry VII in 1499. It was at this point, for some reason, that the annual payment to the Exchequer for 'Cornbury' came to an end.

With the accession of Edward IV we have for the first time for many years a monarch who was a keen lover of hunting. He frequently visited Wychwood and stayed sometimes at Cornbury. There is a romantic legend that he first met his future Queen, Elizabeth Woodville, in Wychwood, when, meeting him supposedly by chance, she threw herself at his feet to ask for the return of her late husband's inheritance. Edward was responsible for the most important attempt for nearly two centuries to reassert royal authority over the whole of the old Hunting Forest, when in 1480, or perhaps earlier, he created 'the King's new Forest within the Forest of Wychwood', stretching from the Evenlode to the Glyme. This divided the old Hunting Forest of Wychwood into two parts, separated by the Evenlode. To keep it under more effective control he gave this new forest its own Ranger, John Fox, who was succeeded in 1482 by Richard Croft. Though it has been said that Richard III disafforested it as soon as he became king, this is unlikely, as appointments to the Rangership of the 'New Forest' continued to be made under the Tudors; it was usually held together with the Keepership of the Royal Park at Woodstock. But there is little evidence that Forest Law was in force there, and the Rangership was probably treated as a profitable sinecure rather than a responsibility. The story of Wychwood Forest from this time on is mainly that of the area south of the Evenlode, centred on Langley and Cornbury.

This presumably is the Forest inherited by the imprisoned Edward Plantagenet. Initially Sir William Norris, of a local family, was appointed to administer it on his behalf, but Richard III appointed Edward Hardgill, who is first mentioned as Ranger in 1468, and may well have been carrying out the duties of the post for all these years in any case. Who looked after Wychwood under Henry VII is unknown: Watney mentions Thomas Croft and Robert Wightill as Rangers, but they were Rangers of the 'New Forest' based on Woodstock. Under Henry VIII, however, Wychwood and Cornbury are united once more, held firstly by Sir William Compton, then Henry Norris, and finally by the Brydges brothers.

The terms of Henry Norris's appointment give for the first time a hint of how the Forest was managed, and how much the officers were paid. In addition to the stewardship of many local manors, Norris was granted 'the offices of four bailiffs in the Forest of Wychwood, alias Eight Walks in Wychwood, with 4d. a day in each office; to be Ranger of Wychwood Forest, with 6d. a day; to be Keeper of Cornbury Park, with 3d. a day.' This is the first reference we have to four bailiwicks and eight walks, though a document of 1332 refers to eight walking foresters and one riding forester [for 'riding forester' see below, p. 54], so we can assume that this structure was an ancient one. It is quite likely that some of those mentioned above as 'rangers' were in fact responsible for only one bailiwick or walk – John Launce in 1416, for example, was paid only 4d. per day – or held the post of riding forester. The Forest would still be divided into eight walks in 1660; by 1792 the number had been reduced to five, each with its own keeper.

Another office, not mentioned here, but found in the Brydges' terms of appointment, was the laundership, with 8d. a day. A 'launde' was an area of grassland from which commoners' cattle were excluded, and which was used to grow hay for the deer. Anthony Fettiplace had been Launder of Burford Launde, perhaps near the present South Lawn Lodge. The Rangers must have gradually accumulated to themselves all the various forest offices, their salaries and perquisites, and then passed on the duties and responsibilities to less well-rewarded deputies. The low rewards for those who actually did the day-to-day work of the Forest contributed much to its decline, as necessity forced them to kill the deer and sell the timber in their care.

We can assume that one lodge was attached to each walk, as a home for its keeper. The first record of named lodges comes in the Woodward's report of 1591, which mentions Potter's Hill Lodge as newly built, and occupied by Thomas Hedgley, keeper. Three other lodges were repaired that year:

1. Shorthampton Lodge, which was occupied by George Rawley, gentleman; this would later be known as Ranger's Lodge. [Was Rawley related to Sir Walter Raleigh? Shorthampton Lodge would later be occupied by another Devon man, Acton Drake, the Earl of Danby's factotum. And if there was a lasting Devon connection, did it have to do with the Forest as a source of naval timber?]
2. 'Newell Lodge' was occupied by Henry Barker; this is probably the one later known as Brize's Lodge, just south of the Leafield-Finstock road.
3. Burford Lodge, the home of Anthony Deverill, Keeper of the Deer.

Other Forest lodges, of which there is no record at this stage, are Waterman's Lodge, High Lodge, also known as Roger's Hill Lodge, and Capp's Lodge on the Burford-Shipton road.

Langley, about which little is known after the demise of the de Langley family, comes back into the picture in Tudor times. The manor had become Crown property and was normally held by the Ranger of the Forest. According to legend, King John had built a palace at Little Langley, but there is little real evidence of this. By 1486, however, a Park had been created there, and a Lodge within it, and these are mentioned several times during the following century. Henry VIII particularly liked Langley; he was there in 1526, and again in 1529 with Bishop Stephen Gardiner. In 1532 he was there with Anne Boleyn, who he would shortly marry, and Sir Francis Weston, who would be executed with her four years later. In 1543 Princess (later Queen) Mary came to Langley to course her greyhounds in the Forest. James I spent three days there in 1605, after which it fell into decay. But the park is recorded on a map in Robert Plot's *The Natural History of Oxfordshire* (1677), and substantial remains were still visible in the late eighteenth century, as Thomas Warton records in his *History of Kiddington* (1782):

> The ruins of King John's Palace, which was inhabited by the royal family until the beginning of Charles I's reign, are still to be seen at the edge of the Forest at a place called Langley. These vestiges of the palace remain: the Queen's garden, park pool, the slaughter-house, the park closes with stone walls ten feet high, a barn and a farmhouse with Gothic arches and windows.

The sixteenth century saw a growing concern about the condition of the royal forests, and various not very successful attempts to reform their management. Henry VII had re-established the Eyre courts in some parts of southern England, but not in Oxfordshire. Surveys ordered by Henry VIII showed that Forest Law was held in contempt, that timber was openly cut down and sold, even by the keepers themselves, that the coppices were not protected, and cattle roamed freely. The lower Forest officials were miserably paid. The re-imposition of Forest Law could be a valuable source of income for an impoverished government, as in the past; but the Law was so decayed that no one really knew how to apply it or where. The Act for the Preservation of Timber, referred to in Chapter 1, was passed in 1543, but had little practical effect. In 1547 posts of Masters and Surveyors of Woods were created, and in 1554 they were replaced by Surveyors-General of Woods, under the authority of the Exchequer. Offences within the Forests could now be prosecuted in the Court of Exchequer Chamber. The authority of the Justices in Eyre declined still further, and even Swanimote courts were held less frequently. This led to the control of the Forests on the ground becoming even weaker. Later in the century fears of a timber famine renewed government concern. Timber was increasingly needed for ship construction, as England's Navy grew, and her merchant enterprisers sailed ever further afield. The end of the sixteenth century was also the time of the 'Great Rebuilding', when new houses went up in towns and villages throughout the land, needing further supplies of good timber.

Ignorance of medieval Forest Law was compounded by a failure to record more recent grants. One of Elizabeth's officials remarked that the Queen ' was too liberal with her gifts before her Majesty knoweth what it is she giveth.' The Earl of Leicester discovered this in 1587, when he tried to ascertain the title to Langley Woods. One John Taverner was asked to enquire into the matter, but found it hard to come up with a clear answer. He reported, *inter alia*, that when a grant of the woods had been made in 1570,

> there were growing in the said coppices vj^c timber oaks valued at vj^s viij^d the piece, which timber oaks were afterwards given by her Majesty to Sir Harry Lee Knight, as I have heard reported, howbeit I never saw any warrant or other gift in writing thereof. Md that the said Forest of Wychwood and the Manor of Langley have always for the space of these lx or iiij^{xx} years been granted together to one person

without any rent paying for the said manor, but whether in respect that the said rent should pay the Keepers their wages I know not.

Robert Dudley, Earl of Leicester, had been assigned Wychwood in 1583 on behalf of his sister-in-law, Anne Countess of Warwick, who was declared of unsound mind in that year. The daughter of the Duke of Somerset, she had married John Dudley, Earl of Warwick, in 1550, when she was granted the tenure of Wychwood for life, which she retained until she died in 1588. Leicester had already held the Manor and Park of Langley since 1580.

When the Countess of Warwick died, the Rangership of the Forest was given to Sir John Fortescue, who already held Cornbury. The grant was made to him and his son Francis, for the term of their lives; and in 1597 he applied to the Queen for the grant to be extended to all his heirs male, and this was done. This would increase the value of the offices if they wanted to sell them, as Francis eventually did. The custody of the Forest and Park was coming to be seen as a piece of private property, like any other leasehold, rather than an appointment in the gift of the Crown.

One way in which Elizabeth's government sought to raise money from the forests was by leasing out the coppices, and in 1596 the eighteen coppices on the royal land in Wychwood were leased for 21 years to Francis Fortescue at an annual rent of £38.18s. The lease gave Fortescue the right to the underwood, but the timber, officially 12 oaks to the acre, remained Crown property. Subsequent occupiers and owners of Cornbury continued to lease the coppices until the nineteenth century on the same terms. This created a conflict of interest which tells us much about the state of the Forest during the coming centuries. Fortescue and his successors had the right to the underwood; but as Rangers they were also responsible to the Crown for the timber. But the more timber trees in the coppices, overshadowing the underwood, the less well the latter would grow. Also, cutting the underwood without damaging the timber trees was not easy, and only too often the latter were damaged, stripped of their side-branches, or felled altogether by wood-cutters wanting to make their job easier and quicker. So in no way did the Ranger have any incentive to care for the Crown's timber. The condition of the coppices did not improve as a result of the lease: in 1617 it was reported that they were in a poor state, much spoiled by the browsing of the deer, and with the fences deliberately removed to allow them access. There was a

Riding between Evenden and Lankeridge copses.

contradiction between effective timber management and the rights of the deer, which would continue until the nineteenth century.

The acreage of the coppices given in Fortescue's lease is 777 acres, the same as in the final lease, for 70 years, to the 4th Duke of Marlborough in 1762. However, when the coppices were surveyed thirteen years later, in 1609, they were found to total 1,564 acres. This is in line with later surveys, for example in 1641 (1,671 acres), in 1792 (1,841 acres) and 1815 (1,649 acres). Every 18 years the underwood in a coppice was cut down and it was re-enclosed. Some extra land might well be included or left out, so small variations are to be expected; but the difference between the figures of 1596 and 1609 can only be explained by the Fortescues deliberately understating the extent of the coppices to reduce the rental cost. That this error remained uncorrected for two centuries, despite several surveys being made in the interval, shows how little real interest the Crown had in the Forests, and how little control it exercised.

The coppices are named in 1596 as: Shakenhofe, Hawkes, Broadquarter, Rowsted, Wastwood, Notridge, Gately and Elyquarter, Kingswood, Leveriche, Smallstone and the Grove, Cockshoothill, Eveden, Great and Little Lankeridge, Hazelwood, Pollard, Buckleap, Five Oak, Slatepits.

Most of these names lasted until the end of the Forest in the 1850s, and in many cases until the present day. Some had been recorded much earlier: Buckleap, Rowsted, Slatepits, Broadquarter and Hazelwood in 1551, and Cockshoothill, Fiveoak, Lankeridge, Notteridge and Smallstones in the thirteenth century. Most of the names probably go back that far.

James I was the first monarch for many years to be an enthusiastic huntsman, and came several times to Wychwood, most notably in 1610, when he was accompanied by his elder son Prince Henry. The heads of the deer they killed are still preserved in the Saloon at Ditchley Park, with lines of doggerel verse on brass plates to show the manner and place of their death. For example:

1610 AUGUST 22ND WEDNESDAY
IN HENLY KNAP TO HUNT ME KING JAMES, PRINCE HENRY
FOUND ME
CORNEBURY PARKE RIVER, TO END THEIR HUNTING,
DROWND ME

At the time there were two places known as Henley Knap – one just south of Enstone, which is still marked on the Ordnance Survey, the other between Leafield and Crawley, which is most probably the one referred to here.

Other inscriptions refer to Foxholes (near Bruern), Kiddington and Rosamund's Well, showing that the King still exercised the right of hunting throughout the whole of the Royal Hunting Forest. Notionally this still existed within its old boundaries, as was shown by a survey of Langley Manor carried out in 1552, which includes the following:

> memo that the lord King has there a forest which pertains to the said manor of Langley called the Forest of Whichewoode...and the limits & bounds of the said forest as follows:

> First from the wall of Woodestoke Park and thence to the bridge called Bladenebrige and so by the water called Bladenbroke [Evenlode] to the water mill of Eynsham and so to le Grymsham and so thence by the rivulet called Wynerusshewater to the bridge of the borough of Burford (reserving the Bishop of Winchester's manor of Whytney with its appurtenances within the said bounds), which extends in length twelve miles, and from the bridge of Burforde by known limits and bounds to the water of Glyme and so thence to the wall of Woodstock Park.

These are the bounds of the Forest as they existed in the thirteenth century, the whole area between the rivers of Glyme, Evenlode and Windrush, and the Gloucestershire border. But the thought that they were still subject to Forest Law would have come as a shock to most of its inhabitants.

Elizabeth's government had sold considerable areas of Crown woodland to raise money, though not in Wychwood, but James's love of hunting made him reluctant to sell any forest land, nor did the growing navy want to lose a valuable source of timber. But the King wanted somehow to get more revenue from the forests, and early in his reign a cunning 'enterpriser' called Otto Nicholson came up with a scheme, which he presented to the King. In medieval times all 'assart' (cleared) land in the forests had been taxed; these taxes had not been paid for years, if not centuries, the ownership of the land had often changed, and the owners had come to treat the land as their own freehold. Nicholson proposed that a survey of all such assart land should be made, and the royal title to it reasserted. Those who believed

themselves to be the owners of the land would be given the choice of buying
the land back from the Crown, compounding for ready money, or paying
an increased rent. If they claimed the land had been theirs, free of rent, for
centuries, the reply was, the greater the loss to the Crown, and the larger
the fine to be paid. Nicholson's scheme met with royal approval, and he was
appointed head of a commission to put it into practice, taking a percentage
of all the money received.

Nicholson's survey of Wychwood was carried out in 1609, and gives
detailed information about landholding, and also maps of each coppice in
the royal woodlands. 1725 acres of assart land were 'discovered', producing
nearly £450 in fines; this was much less than in some other counties. The
manors most affected were those near Woodstock which were notionally
part of Edward IV's 'New Forest', but had been described in 1596 as
'within the old precinct of the Forest of Wychwood, but not used or
regarded as parcel of the same within the memory of man.' It was bad
enough for the freeholders to have to pay rental for their own land; but then
in 1610 an Eyre court was held in Woodstock, at which the Chief Justice
ordered a new perambulation and included them in a new Forest bailiwick
of Woodstock. Sir Henry Lee, Ranger of Woodstock, brought in red and
fallow deer and seized some common land for their pasture; the deer broke
out and damaged their crops; the freemen were forced to serve on
Swanimote juries, or fined for their absence; they were injured in their rights
of vert and venison; and some were even sent to London in custody, for
felling trees on their own lands. All these complaints appeared in a petition
to Parliament in 1617 from the indignant inhabitants of 'the several town-
ships of Wotton, Hordley, Oulde Woodstocke, Bladon, Stonefield,
Coombe and Handborough, adjoyning to his ma^ties manor house of
Woodstocke'.

By now Nicholson's scheme had been wound up, having raised over
£25,000 throughout England, and maybe this had given them the courage
to approach Parliament. The protest seems to have had an effect, as in 1622
another perambulation of the Forest was made, and its boundaries were
finally restricted to the old royal demesne land, stretching from Cornbury
to the Shipton-Swinbrook road.

It is from about this time that we find the first references to the 'Purlieu',
but whether it was created now or earlier remains very uncertain. A Purlieu
consisted of an area adjoining a Forest, which had once been part of it, and

where the King's deer still had the right to wander and were hunted. To watch over them a new office had been created, that of Riding Forester, or sometimes Ranger – and this may be the origin of the latter title. (As we can see below, Danby's deputy Acton Drake is referred to as a Riding Forester in the 1630s.) The Purlieu of Wychwood included three coppices to the north of the Forest, Knighton, Boynal and Priestgrove, a number of coppices at the western end, stretching almost as far as Capp's Lodge and Swinbrook; and the whole area to the south, almost as far as Minster Lovell and Crawley, but excluding Leafield. (See map on p. 116.) In compensation for the inconvenience and damage caused by the deer, landowners in the Purlieu were granted a certain number of deer carcasses each year, known as 'composition venison'; this continued to be supplied until the final disappearance of the Forest in the mid-nineteenth century.

It might have seemed that the perambulation of 1622 had finally put to rest the old Royal Hunting Forest of Wychwood. However, when Charles I came to the throne he made a far more extensive attempt to raise money, firstly by reviving in 1632 the whole apparatus of ancient Forest Law and administration, and later by extending the Forest bounds once more to their old limits. The old Forest Courts were ordered to meet again, and, somewhat incredibly, a Regard was ordered into 'all assarts, wastes and purprestures since the second year after the first coronation of Henry III' – i.e.1218. Those ordered to attend included all forest officers, free tenants living in the Forest, a reeve and four men from each forest village, and all those accused of offences – over, presumably, a period of 400 years. Great crowds gathered at the courthouses – in Northamptonshire the Puritan Lord Edward Montagu was reminded of Ezra X. 13: 'But the people are many, and it is a time of much rain, and we are not able to stand without, neither is this a work of one day or two: for we are many that have transgressed in this thing.'

In Wychwood the Court House was near Five Oak coppice. The sensation caused by such a large gathering was still remembered 150 years later, when James Smith, the Billman of the Forest, told a Parliamentary Commission how he had heard from his father that 'formerly the Forest Courts were held in a house where Five Oaks Pound now stands.' Three Swanimote Courts were held in 1635 and 1636, followed by a Forest Eyre in Oxford in 1637. The Swanimotes were presided over by the Earl of

Danby as Lieutenant of the Forest, the Verderers, Sir Francis Wenman and John Fettiplace, and Acton Drake, who is described as Principal Ranger of the Forest, Riding Forester, and Forester of Shorthampton Walk. Drake, who as we have seen was handsomely remembered in Danby's will, was the true manager of the Forest.

The revival of the Forest Courts may in the end have been a futile exercise, but their records do gave a rare snapshot of actual conditions at the time – the exploitation of the Forest resources by those who were supposed to care for them, the poor condition of the coppices unprotected from deer and cattle, and the frequent invasions by the inhabitants of the local villages seizing what they could for firewood.

A major offender was an earlier Ranger called Anthony Cook. (The title of Ranger must mean that he was Danby's deputy, and probably Drake's predecessor. Danby, we see from these documents, is called the Lieutenant of the Forest.) Cook had, perhaps conveniently, died some six years before; but, it was noted, 'Silvester Cook was Brother and next Heir of the said Anthony' and thus liable to pay the fines imposed. Cook had 'permitted his beasts to wander and depasture' in several coppices, and had also 'licensed certain of his servants to keep and pasture divers of their Cattle in certain Coppices…called Lankridge Grove and Evenden then enclosed being in great deterioration…and afterwards the aforesaid Coppices were almost wholly destroyed by the Beasts of the Commons wandering and depasturing the same for want of fences.' Cook had also 'cut down 50 Oak Trees within the demesne of the Forest…in destruction of the Vert.'

But this was little compared with the depredations of his superiors. Sir Robert Howard, son of the Duke of Somerset, and Robert Vaux, had dug up 2000 roots and stools of trees; Sir Francis Stonor had cut down and sold 400 of the King's trees some 40 years before; Sir Francis Fortescue had cut down and sold 500 trees 25 years before, while the Forest was in his custody; Danby himself, who was presiding over the Court, had 'cut down 100 Trees called Dottard Trees…carried them away and used them for firewood.' He was fined £200, while the heir of Francis Stonor had to pay £1500.

As for the activities of the poor, the court noted the tearing down of coppice hedges by 'certain men' in Asthall Wood, so that the Vert of the said coppice was entirely destroyed. Hawkes and Broadquarter coppices had also been 'deteriorated' by the poor of Burford and Fulbrook 'to the

The Kennels (early twentieth century).

Annual Value of ten pounds'. And Richard Harris, presumably a Regarder, 'presented that divers paupers of the Forest Inhabitants were common malefactors in the Vert of the same Forest.'

Some seemingly legitimate actions by the Rangers were also brought before the court, presumably because formal permission had not been granted. Anthony Cook had cut down 70 trees to repair Shorthampton Lodge, build a new barn, and repair gates to the coppices. Acton Drake was fined a token 20 pence because he had

> built and erected a certain House upon the demesne soil of the Forest...the aforesaid House from the time of the erection thereof thitherto had been and was then used for receiving the Dogs of Chace within the Forest and the new erection of the House was against the laws and assize of the Forest and to the damage to the King of one shilling whereof nothing was answered to the King.

This 'house' was the Kennels, near Buckleap Copse. Originally built for deerhounds, it would be revived in the eighteenth century for foxhounds, and would finally become a set of cottages for estate workers, still keeping the same name.

Another detail of the decayed state of the Forest was the large number of Cony-boroughs (rabbit warrens), especially in the north-western area of the Forest, from Shorthampton to Burford Launde (South Lawn) 'to the great damage to the Vert of the Forest to the value of ten pounds and to the super burthen of the Pasture and Herbage there and to the damage of the Lord the King in his hunting there…'

The second royal device for getting money out of the forests was to increase their size. There were rumours that the whole of England would be turned into Forest except for the counties of Kent, Surrey and Sussex. Compared with that the King's actions were quite modest: in 1638 all the manors around Wychwood that had been part of the Forest in the thirteenth century were now declared to be a new Forest. This repeated, on a larger scale, the action of Edward IV 150 years before. The decree implies that these areas had never ceased to be part of the Forest, but that 'by reason they lie remote from the lodges of the foresters of Wychwood Forest, have been neglected, and due care has not been taken of the deer and vert there.' They would now be known as 'The New Bailiwick of the honour of Woodstock within the Forest of Wychwood for ever', and the Earl of Pembroke was appointed its Lieutenant. The aim was to persuade the landowners to pay large fines to be released from the Regard; but by 1641 the Earl of Pembroke had sided with Parliament and lost all his offices, and the King was forced to accept the Perambulation of 1622.

The boundaries of Wychwood were finally settled, but the conflict between the needs of the deer and cattle, and preservation of the timber, remained unresolved. Earlier concerns about the timber seem to have faded and it was still the deer that the Government cared about most. In 1631 Danby was paid £455 4s 2d to build a wall round both Cornbury and Wychwood 'for the preservation of his Majesty's game'. Since in 1606 £245 had been allocated for walling an extension to Cornbury Park, the sum hardly seems enough for a wall around the whole Forest. However, in this case the King, through Danby, would only be responsible for the actual building of the wall; neighbouring landowners had to dig the stone, and their tenants carry it to the site. This was related to the ancient tradition of 'hedge-acre' and 'wall-acre', by which landowners were allowed a 24-yard-wide strip of underwood within a neighbouring coppice, in return for keeping the coppice boundary in good repair. In the present instance, the new wall would protect their lands from the deer. As we can see from the accounts for the Cornbury wall in 1611, digging and carriage of the stone made up more than three-quarters of the total cost.

The wall took a long time to build, since we find Cromwell ordering its completion in 1655. The following year the Treasury Commissioners reported: 'The wall will cost the State £700 to finish on the former conditions, viz.: the owners of inheritance-lands to dig the stone, the tenants to carry it.' It was partly financed by the sale of dotard trees to the value of £200, and this time it must have been completed. At the end of the eighteenth century it was reported that the Forest 'was almost entirely encompassed with a stone wall' which also included some of the private lands within the Purlieu. This made it unique among the Royal Forests of England.

It is perhaps unexpected that the Commonwealth government should show as much concern about the deer as had its royal predecessors. Cromwell had ordered the completion of the wall 'for better preservation and increase of the deer'. Three years later the Council, hearing that some deer had been killed, ordered the Rangers 'strictly to preserve the deer, and allow no warrants to kill and deliver save from Parliament or the Council, and to look well after the grass and meadow lands that there may be winter provision for them.' In 1655 Cromwell, just like a medieval monarch, ordered bucks and roes from the Forest to be sent to his friend John Dutton at Sherbourne, to stock his new Park.

Philip Pettit has commented that the revival of Forest Law by Charles had in fact killed it off, and that after the Restoration it was a 'mere antiquarian survival'. Neither the Commonwealth nor any subsequent government developed a policy for managing the timber in the Royal Forests, and the story of the following two centuries is one of continuing neglect and exploitation, to be exposed by a series of official enquiries in the late eighteenth and nineteenth centuries. It has been estimated that during the Napoleonic War the Crown forests, properly managed, could have satisfied all the needs of the Royal Navy; yet they only provided 7.5% of naval timber, the rest coming from private woods (68%) and imports. This was a problem which had to wait for the energy and reforming spirit of a later age before it would be addressed.

6

The Earls of Clarendon and Rochester

With the restoration of the monarchy in 1660, Cornbury and Wychwood passed into the hands of the great statesman and historian, Edward Hyde, Earl of Clarendon. Not only is he the most distinguished of all the historical figures to have lived there, but it was he who commissioned the rebuilding of Cornbury House in virtually its present form.

Hyde was a successful lawyer who had been born to a gentry family in Wiltshire in 1609. Elected to Parliament in 1640, by the autumn of 1641 he had become the effective leader of the royal party in the Commons. He was a 'constitutional royalist', who tried to persuade the King to avoid unconstitutional action, and take a stand upon his legal rights. With the start of the Civil War he was expelled from the Commons, and spent the years 1642 to 1645 with the King at Oxford. In 1643 Charles I appointed him a Privy Councillor and Chancellor of the Exchequer, but later his influence declined, as the King listened more to those who spoke for all-out war, rather than Hyde's policy of compromise and concession

The King still had enough confidence in him, however, to entrust the Prince of Wales to his care, and in 1645 he and the Prince went to the West of England. From there they fled before the victorious Fairfax, first to the Scilly Isles, and afterwards to Jersey, where the 15-year-old Charles fathered the first of his many illegitimate children. In 1646 Queen Henrietta Maria ordered the Prince to join her in Paris; Hyde and his Council advised him not to go, for fear that under the Queen's influence he would become a Catholic. This advice was ignored by the Prince, and made the Queen Hyde's bitter enemy. He remained in Jersey, and there he began writing his

Edward Hyde, 1st Earl of Clarendon. From a portrait by Jordaens.

famous *History of the Rebellion,* an account of his times which is one of the first major historical works in English. In 1648, with the outbreak of the Second Civil War, he left Jersey and joined the Queen and Prince in Paris, and for the next twelve years he remained with them in exile. The Prince, clearly recognising his qualities, retained him as a councillor despite the Queen's hostility, and he was formally appointed Lord Chancellor in 1658.

Over the next two years he superintended the negotiations which finally led to the restoration of Charles to the throne in May 1660.

He had the King's support, but the Queen and many of the other exiles were bitterly hostile to him. His strong commitment to Anglicanism made both Catholics and Presbyterians his enemies, and on the eve of the Restoration the Queen and General Monk both tried to exclude him from power, but to no avail. Hyde accompanied Charles II on his triumphal entry to London on May 29th, and three days later he was confirmed as Chancellor, and in effect head of the government. His policy was to encourage Charles in the spirit of compromise and tolerance which had allowed his restoration, and to oppose those Royalists who sought revenge on their opponents.

At the coronation in April 1661 he was created Earl of Clarendon and Viscount Cornbury, and in August the King gave him Cornbury Park, and appointed him to 'Le Eight Walkes' and the Rangership and Laundership 'in Foresta Nostra de Wichwood'. Clarendon, near Salisbury, was also a Royal Forest, in which Hyde had some financial interest, but it was Cornbury that he chose as his main country residence. As overseer of Danby's Will, he must have been familiar with it, and may well have had his eye on it for many years. Like his predecessors, he leased the 18 coppices within the Forest, and was granted the manors of Langley, Leafield and Ramsden; and 'Newfrith, alias Brice's Lodge', which had belonged to Danby and had been forfeited by Sir John Danvers. Sir John's widow had to make do with land in Shorthampton and Chilson.

Clarendon also became Lord Lieutenant of Oxfordshire, and Chancellor of Oxford University, which he did much to restore after the disturbances of the Civil War and Commonwealth. The name of Clarendon has since become almost synonymous with the University, and he is commemorated in, among others, the Clarendon Building, the Clarendon Laboratory and the Clarendon Press.

The years of exile had not been easy for Hyde, or for the rest of the exiled court, as his letters show: 'At this time I have neither clothes nor fire to preserve me from the sharpness of the season.' 'I am so cold that I am scarce able to hold my pen, and have not three sous in the world to buy a faggot.' Now that he had both power and prosperity he was determined to enjoy them. He started building a palatial home, Clarendon House, in Piccadilly, next to Burlington House. Designed by Roger Pratt, it would eventually cost £50,000. This was the original home of his famous collection of portraits, which he had begun even before the Restoration. Such collections, displayed in a Long Gallery, had become fashionable, and Clarendon's were mainly of statesmen he had known, whose actions were described in his History. Many years later John Evelyn wrote to Samuel Pepys that Clarendon's purpose was:

> to furnish all the rooms of state and other apartments with the pictures of the most illustrious of our nation, especially of his Lordship's time and acquaintance, and of divers before it.

These were figures distinguished in church and state, military affairs and the law, but also

> what was most agreeable to his Lordship's general humour, old Chaucer, Shakespeare, Beaumont and Fletcher (who were both in one piece) Spenser, Mr Waller, Cowley, Hudibras, which last he placed in the room where he used to eat and dine in public.

As the most powerful man in England after the King, he had no difficulty in getting hold of what he wanted. Evelyn again:

> when his design was made known, anybody who either had them of their own, or could purchase them at any price, strove to make their court by these presents; by which means he got many excellent pieces of Vandyke, and other originals by Lely and the best of our modern masters' hands.

A catalogue of the collection made in the eighteenth century lists 22 Vandykes and 9 Lelys, as well as a few 'after Vandyke', but most are probably copies, or painted by assistants. Clarendon's interest was not in the artists, but in the sitters and their historical significance. In 1683 the collection was taken from Clarendon House to Cornbury, where it remained for nearly a century.

In 1663 Clarendon was at the peak of his career. The Countess of Devonshire met him in August and wrote, 'My Lord Chancellor goes to Cornbury, and stays there till Michaelmas. He did me the honour to come take his leave of me. I never saw him merrier nor look better, and I believe never had more reason.' That autumn the King and Queen visited Cornbury, on their way to Oxford.

23rd of September being Wednesday, the King and Queen, with their royal highnesses the duke and duchess of York, came from Cirencester to dine with the Lord Chancellor at Cornberry. The vice-cancellor sent Mr. Bland, the glover, to Cornberry to observe that as soone as the king was set down to dinner, to come away to Oxon to give notice to the vice-cancellor and the Doctors of it.

The University dignitaries, thus forewarned, welcomed the royal party at a quarter past six that evening. Two days later the King and his brother went hunting in Wychwood and returned to Cornbury to stay the night.

The improvement of Cornbury was Clarendon's second great project, after the building of Clarendon House. It was the Park that first had his attention. According to Robert Plot, in his *Natural History of Oxfordshire* (1677), it had not been well cared for during the Commonwealth, and was overrun with rabbits, which had had a strange effect on the deer:

Nor can I pass without admiration, the deer of Cornbury Park, which before His Majesty's wonderful Restoration, being (in part at least) turned into a Conywarren, the Deer upon it had all Dwarf-heads, the most of them irregular...but if any of them were uniform...yet they were still far short of growth, seldom exceeding 8 or 10 Inches long, though the Deer themselves were well-enough grown, and warrantable; – which yet, as soon as the Warren was destroyed by the Proprietor, the Right Honourable the Earl of Clarendon, came again to have as fair Branched-Heads as any Deer whatever in the adjoining Forrest: Which strange Alterations I cannot guess to proceed from any other Cause, that the Infection of the Grass by the Urine and Crotising of the Conies, which being Hot and Dry must needs abate the Moisture of the Deer.

Clarendon not only destroyed rabbit-warrens, but laid out the Park with great avenues of oak, beech and lime, and quincunx patterns of fir and mountain pine. Plot would later write: 'Of walks, the most curious I have met with in this county, are those elegant ones of trees of various kinds in Cornbury Park.' In February 1663 Clarendon wrote to his sons with detailed instructions about the planting of trees that he had just ordered:

However I pray lett all the holes be digged that the Gardyner may plant the trees as they come: for I suppose there will be a fortnight's

John Evelyn.

time to sett in after you returne ... If you think fitt, lett Hugh May sett out four rounde or square places in which the Gardyner may be appointed to sett all manner of seedes ... of Ashe, Walnutte, Haslenutts, Acornes and the like, which in 3 or 4 yeares will be a fyne thicket, and in a little more tyme will be copses. I am sure you do not forgett to sett all the lyme trees which were kept togither in the garden when I was ther.

The new design of the Park owed much to John Evelyn, a close friend of his son, who in addition to his fame as a diarist was an enthusiastic proponent of tree-planting. The Civil War and its aftermath had led to a great destruction of timber, as so much wood was needed to rebuild what had been destroyed. Cromwell's government had also made a point of felling the timber in the parks of their enemies as a way of punishing them. Evelyn was commissioned by the Royal Society to encourage the planting of trees and lecture on the subject; the result of this was his book *Sylva, or a Discourse on Forest Trees*, published in 1662. Here he laments 'the inexhaustible magazine of timber, destroyed by Cromwellian rebels, through all England...let us arise then and plant, and not give over till we have repaired the havoc our barbarous enemies have made.' So he must have been delighted in 1664 to be invited to Cornbury to design the planting of the Park. He recorded the visit in his diary:

> Oct. 17th. I went with My Lo. Visct. Cornbury [Clarendon's eldest son] to Cornbury in Oxfordshire, to assist him in the planting of the Park, and beare him company, with Mr. Belin and Mr. May, in a coach with 6 horses; dined at Uxbridge, lay at Wicckam [Wycombe]. 18th. At Oxford. Went thro' Woodstock, where we beheld the destruction of that royal seate and park by ye late rebels, and arriv'd that evening at Cornbury, an house lately built by the Earle of Denbigh [Danby] on ye middle of a sweete park, wall'd with a dry wall. The house is of excellent freestone abounding in that part, a stone that is fine, but never sweats or casts any damp; 'tis of ample dimensions, has goodly cellars, the paving of ye hall admirable for its close laying. We design'd an handsom chapell that was yet wanting; as Mr. May had the stables, which indeed are very faire, having set out the walkes in the park and gardens. The lodge is a pretty solitude, and the ponds very convenient; the park well stor'd.

In *Sylva* Evelyn suggests that a park could be a pleasure ground, and not just a chase for deer, and his idea of 'forest gardening' was first put into practice at Cornbury.

The Hugh May referred to in the last two quotations was Clarendon's architect for the alterations at Cornbury. He and Roger Pratt were the leading architects of the early Restoration period, and between them they

The stable block.

determined the new direction of domestic architecture in England. 'It was their achievement,' according to John Newman, 'by drawing on their continental experiences during the years of Civil War and Interregnum, to naturalise [Inigo] Jones's classicism among the English aristocracy and gentry.' May was Commissioner for the Repairs of St Paul's, and Paymaster-General of the King's Works, and built several important houses, including Berkeley House in Piccadilly, and Cassiobury in Hertfordshire. As with Danby's architect Nicholas Stone, the main influences on his work were Dutch. He had shared the court's exile in Holland, where he had been greatly struck by the new style of domestic architecture developed by van Campen, designer of the Mauritshuis in The Hague. The form is that of a simple block with a central pediment, and a hipped roof with dormers. May introduced this style into England, first employing it at the much smaller Eltham Lodge in Kent, completed in 1663. For more than a century it would dominate country house building: as it had thirty years before, Cornbury led the way in architectural fashion.

May's initial commission was to design the stables, which had been completed by the time of his visit with Evelyn in 1664. The stable block, separated from the main house by the stable yard, today faces the drive and is the main building visible from the entrance gates. It had stalls and horse-boxes at each end and a coach house in the middle, above which were rooms for male servants. On the north side there was a long riding school,

The chapel.

open to the roof. Clarendon believed that riding was an important part of a gentleman's education, and proposed (without success) the building of a similar school at Oxford University.

The stables, as we can see in the quotation above from Evelyn's diary, were followed by a new Chapel. It has long been believed that the Chapel was not built until 1677, but John Newman has shown clearly that building started immediately after the completion of the stables. A letter of 1666 to his Oxfordshire agent John Cary shows Clarendon's detailed concern about the paving:

> The best couler and the best grained Stone, which is neither the light nor the darke but the middle blewish Stone, and all of the same, and to be layed Diamond wise all of a Size with a border round the Chappell al of one couler, and not to intermixe coulers.

The stone was from Langley. It was known as 'Forest Marble', and Robert Plot describes it as

> wholly composed of a close union of Cockles, scarce any of them

exceeding a pea in bigness, and streaked circularly to the hinges of the valves, they are none of them hollow, but firmer within, than they are to the bed of stone where they lye; and yet even to that they are so closely knit, that the mass receives a very good polish, insomuch that his Lordship intends to pave the new Chappel now building at Cornbury with it.

Somewhat like a small College chapel, it has a rich plaster ceiling, and a gallery at one end, beneath which is a wooden screen and gates carved with openwork scrolls and foliage. Along the side walls are pews and a pulpit, and the panels of the reredos are decorated with carved swags of flowers, once believed to be the work of Grinling Gibbons. Above there is a large shield with the Clarendon arms. It has, writes Jennifer Sherwood, 'the best late C17 interior in the county outside Oxford. It is also of national importance as a rare example of a private chapel of this date.'

By August 1667 the Chapel had been paved, and major alterations begun on the main house, with a new east wing built at least to roof level. Known as the Clarendon wing, this is a larger version of Eltham Lodge, with four window bays on each side of a three-bay central feature with Corinthian pilasters and a pediment. The windows are sashed, with bold glazing bars. The cornice, which projects two foot six inches, allowing for a wide lead gutter, runs round the whole of the east and south wings. Danby's south wing was altered by May to conform with the new building: a first floor was inserted into the Great Hall, and first floor sash windows and a hipped roof with dormers added. These alterations have made it impossible to know what the Danby wing originally looked like; and the disappearance of the Great Hall shows the change in the life-style of the aristocracy that had come about with the Restoration. Clarendon would not dine with his whole household as Danby had done. But the plasterwork of Danby's ceiling was preserved in the new rooms created above.

On the fascia of the cornice, under the pediment of the new wing, is a quotation from Virgil: 'Deus nobis haec otia fecit' (A god has made this place of leisure for us). This line, spoken by the shepherd Tityrus in the First Eclogue, expresses Virgil's gratitude to the Emperor Augustus for his patronage, and for returning to him the ancestral estate from which he had been exiled. Like Augustus, Charles had brought peace to his land after a long civil war, and had granted the Cornbury estate to the once exiled Clarendon.

The south-east, or Clarendon, wing.

With this inscription, Clarendon both paid a profound compliment to Charles II and marked the beginning of England's own Augustan Age.

Finally, terrace walls were built around the House. These were originally built in stone from the park, which proved unsuitable, and they had to be rebuilt in Taynton stone. Although the word 'Ha-ha' for a sunken wall would not be invented until the following century, Cornbury's terrace wall has the same effect – to allow an open view across the park while keeping the deer away.

Hugh May was an architect of a very different breed to Nicholas Stone. Stone had begun life as a mason, and took a hands-on approach to his work at Cornbury, visiting 33 times during the construction. Hugh May was a gentleman and courtier, who left even the drawing of detailed plans to subordinates, and supervised the work mainly by letter from London. Clarendon himself also sent detailed advice about the building to his Oxfordshire agent John Cary, and it was probably Cary who supervised most of the work. Cary was a man of some importance locally: a lawyer, he was agent for the Ditchley estate as well as Cornbury and was rich enough to buy the Wilcote estate for himself in 1667. In 1675 he bought a large house in the High Street in Woodstock, where he would entertain the King himself, William III, in 1695.

The builder was another of the Strongs of Barrington, Thomas, the grandson of Timothy Strong who had worked for Danby. He would later become Clerk of Works under Wren in the rebuilding of St. Paul's. The stone came from the Cornbury quarry near Buckleap Copse, which was possibly first opened by Nicholas Stone. It is an exceptionally fine, hard-wearing building stone, that weathers to a deep yellow shade. In 1948 this stone was identified by W.J.Arkell as an Inferior Oolitic Limestone known as Clypeus Grit, so-called because it is full of fragments of fossil sea-urchins or sand-dollars (Clypeus). Clypeus Grit is common in the local stonebrash fields, and is normally useless as building material, but at Cornbury there is a unique development of freestone at the top of the Clypeus Grit bed in a layer up to 5 feet thick. This stone has been used for all building at Cornbury since the seventeenth century, and was also used in the building of Blenheim Palace.

In January 1666 Lord Cornbury wished Evelyn could pay another visit.

If you had not more important affairs upon your hands, you should have been dragged ere this by importunity to Cornbury, to finish the work you have begun, whither I go now and then upon a Saturday; my little boy Edward there, and that place, are too many enjoyments at this time, when one ought not to indulge oneself. I cannot tell you how to admiration things go on there; we have this year planted near two thousand trees... Mr. May (who you know governs at Cornbury) hath made a design for a very convenient house there, and splendid enough, which will be begun this spring; and then we shall be very commodious in both town and country, though perhaps too much envied.

That last phrase shows that the son was perhaps wiser than his father, for Clarendon's extravagance in building was one of the reasons why public sentiment turned against him and led to his downfall. His position was far less secure that it may have appeared, and there were always enemies at court ready to accuse him of corruption or treason. Back in 1660 had come the revelation of his daughter Anne's secret marriage to the King's brother, James Duke of York. Neither he nor the King was aware of it, and when Clarendon was told, according to his own account, 'he broke out into very immoderate passion against the wickedness of his daughter,' advised the

King to imprison her in the Tower for her presumption, and even said he would consent to her execution. The easy-going Charles, however, was ready enough to accept Anne as his sister-in-law, and assured the Chancellor that 'his daughter was a woman of great wit and excellent parts', would take good advice from her father, and exert a beneficial influence over her husband. But others in the Royal family were enraged. The King's eldest sister, the Princess of Orange, declared she would never yield precedence to someone who had been her waiting-woman. The Queen Mother, Henrietta Maria, threatened to leave the Palace as soon as Anne entered it, though she was eventually persuaded to yield. The marriage connected Clarendon closely with the Royal Family, and would make him the grandfather of two monarchs, Mary II and Anne; but it did not help him with those who were already jealous of his power and despised him for his humble origins.

He had made another powerful enemy in the King's favourite mistress, Barbara Villiers, Lady Castlemaine, by refusing to visit her, or affix the Great Seal to any grant in her favour. She represented the King's addiction to an easy, self-indulgent life, which Clarendon, familiar with the stricter court of Charles I, strongly disapproved of. By 1667 his position had grown much weaker. Public affairs had not prospered. England had been humiliated when the Dutch sailed up the Medway and burned the fleet at Chatham. Even though he had opposed the Dutch War the Commons turned against him; and numerous accusations of corruption gained credit from his too visible expenditure on Clarendon House. He had tactlessly carried on building it despite the Plague and the Fire, which infuriated the suffering Londoners. The failure of the King to produce an heir was, rather unfairly, also held against him, as it made his son-in-law James the next in the line of succession. Having lost the favour of both Court and Commons, Clarendon was a natural scapegoat for a series of public disasters, and Charles came under enormous pressure from those closest to him to dismiss his Chancellor.

Then on August 9th Frances, his wife of 33 years, died. This was, he wrote, 'so sudden, unexpected and irreparable a loss that he had not the courage to support; which nobody wondered at who knew the mutual satisfaction and comfort they had in each other.' Charles came to condole with him, but nevertheless decided the time had come to remove him from office. On August 30th the King sent for the Great Seal, and Clarendon was dismissed. The Commons then moved towards impeachment. One of the charges was that 'he had alienated lands from the Crown, particularly Clarendon and Cornbury,' and, in more general terms, 'that he hath, in short time, gained to himself a greater estate than can be imagined to be lawfully gained in so short a time; and contrary to his oath, procured several grants, under the Great Seal, from his Majesty, to himself and his relations, of several of his majesty's lands, hereditaments and leases.' Lady Castlemaine said she would not be happy until she saw his head on a stake.

Had Clarendon left London for Cornbury the crisis might have blown over. Insisting on defending himself, but also perhaps paralysed by grief for his wife, he stayed in London. In November Evelyn paid his last visit.

> I found him in his garden at his new-built Palace, sitting in his gout wheel-chair, and seeing the gates setting up towards the north and the fields. He looked and spoke very disconsolately. After some while deploring his condition to me, I took my leave. Next morning I heard he was gone; though I am persuaded, that, had he gone sooner, though but to Cornbury, and there lain quiet, it would have satisfied the Parliament. That which exasperated them was his presuming to stay and contest the accusation so long as it was possible, and they were on the point of sending him to the Tower.

For fear of the Commons Charles would not give him a passport to leave the country, but on November 29th he privately told Clarendon to escape. That same evening he took a farmer's boat to Calais. Shortly after he had further evidence of his unpopularity when he met a party of English sailors who were owed many months' pay in England, and accused him of embezzling it. They attacked him brutally and he was lucky to escape with his life.

He had left behind a written self-defence, which was presented to the House of Lords; but it was named a 'scandalous and seditious paper' and burned by the public hangman. A bill was passed for his banishment, and his return was made high treason.

The remaining seven years of his life were passed in exile, where he completed his *History*. He would never see his new house at Cornbury, but he had not forgotten it. In 1671 he wrote to his son:

> I cannot but still put you in mind of Cornbury, to the care whereof methinks your own concernment should invite you, and to make all things handsome for your own reception. I am sure, if what I

assigned for that purpose had been laid out on it, since I came away, much would have been done; at least, all things would have been clean; and I pray you tell me what is done there, and how near all the new building is made inhabitable; and I hope you and your wife, and all your company, will spend at least one month together at Cornbury this summer, and then I shall think you will indeed take some care of it.

Shortly before his death he wrote to the King and Queen, pleading that he should be allowed to die in his own country and among his children, but had no reply. He died in Rouen on December 9th, 1674. In death he was allowed to return, and was buried in Westminster Abbey.

He was succeeded as Earl of Clarendon, and owner of Cornbury, by his eldest son Henry. With the courtesy title of Lord Cornbury, Henry had been M.P. for Wiltshire since 1661; in the Commons he was always loyal to his father's interests, and throughout his life he never wavered in his support of the Stuart family, and the Church of England. But his real interests lay outside politics, for which he had little taste or skill. He was a Fellow of the Royal Society, and wrote a history of Winchester Cathedral. He loved gardening, and was always fond of Cornbury. In 1662 he wrote to his sister-in-law Lady Worcester about his eagerness to leave London:

I may do what I will till Michaelmas, and by the grace of God I will make what haste I can into the country, it is much better walking in the park at Cornbury than in a gallery here. I have not yet been here a week, and really I am quite weary of the Court already. Do you not think then I am like to make an excellent good courtier? I know you will not believe me, but God willing I intend to be very speedily at Cornbury.

As Earl of Clarendon, however, and brother-in-law of James, Duke of York, he could not escape public life. In 1680 he became a Privy Councillor, the Queen's Treasurer, and Keeper of Somerset House. Twice he entertained his royal relatives at Cornbury. In 1681 King Charles came to stay the night after watching a horse race at Burford; and two years later the Duke of York and his new Duchess Mary of Modena (Anne Hyde had died in 1671), together with Princess Anne, stayed for a weekend.

It was about this time that James asked Clarendon to appoint Colonel

Henry Hyde, Viscount Cornbury (later 2nd Earl of Clarendon) and his first wife Theodosia Capel in 1662. From a portrait by Lely.

John Legge to the post of Deputy Ranger of Wychwood, in succession to his brother Richard Legge. As protegés of Danby, the Legges had long been associated with Cornbury. John Legge survived to the age of 109, and was buried at Charlbury in 1702. 'He remembered the death of Queen Elizabeth. He had great vivacity to the last, and great strength of body, lived always cheerfully and freely, and died at last not through any decay of nature, but by wilful letting of blood contrary to physician's advice.' At the time of his appointment he would have been nearly 90, and this suggests that even a lesser Forest Office had become a perquisite rather than a post of responsibility. (A later reference makes clear that Legge had only been granted one of the Walks in the Forest.)

With the Duke of York's accession as James II Clarendon's political responsibilities increased. He became Lord Privy Seal, and at the end of 1685 was sent to Ireland as Lord-Lieutenant. His younger brother Laurence, Earl of Rochester, was Lord High Treasurer, and James hoped to persuade both of them to become Catholics, sending priests to argue with them, but in vain. After two painful years in Ireland, where he was treated with contempt by Catholic peasants and Presbyterian colonists alike, he was dismissed in 1687, together with his brother. It was a humiliation, but also to some extent a relief. 'Indeed I think it is time to leave off thoughts of having to do with the world', he wrote to Laurence. The King gave him a pension of £2000 a year, and he retired from official life. The Hyde brothers had been loyal servants of James since youth, and the sole reason for their dismissal was their religion. Evelyn wrote,

> It was very hard, and looked very unkindly, his Majesty (as my Lord Clarendon protested to me) finding not the least failure of duty in him during his government of that kingdom [Ireland] so that his recall plainly appeared to be from the stronger influence of the Papists...

While Clarendon was in Ireland, Cornbury had been occupied by one of his father's oldest friends, the Duke of Ormonde. He had replaced the elder Clarendon as Chancellor of Oxford, and while at Cornbury held 'a great Court', and received formal visits from the Vice-chancellor and heads of houses – 'as many as would fill three coaches with six horses apiece'.

Now retired, Clarendon could enjoy Cornbury more. In March 1688 his diary records a ten-day visit with his brother. On Sundays he went to church in Charlbury, he visited the Jenkinsons at Walcot, entertained young officers quartered at Oxford, and rode in the Forest. In August he returned with his family, and welcomed a succession of friends. It was in this year that he built the high wall between the stable block and the east wing, perhaps the walled kitchen gardens, and a new bridge over the Evenlode. Watney believed this was the bridge that now leads to the main entrance, which is recorded on a map of 1761; but there is also another bridge, now disused, a few hundred yards downstream. This carried a road from Cornbury House up to the Woodstock Road near Lee's Rest, and was in use until the building of the railway in 1853. It has also been suggested that the main entrance to the Park had originally been from the north-west, near Ranger's Lodge.

Political events were moving swiftly towards the crisis of the Glorious Revolution, and William of Orange's arrival with his army was widely expected. At the beginning of September Clarendon left Cornbury for London; both he and his brother wished to show themselves at Court to avoid suspicion. But keeping loyal, both to his Anglican faith and to his

Catholic King, was not easy. At a meeting of the Council, he refused to sit at the same table with a Catholic priest, and later he attacked the King's policy of raising a Catholic regiment for his personal guard. Then he heard that his son, Lord Cornbury, had gone over to William with his regiment of dragoons – the first to defect. He was appalled:

> O God, that my son should be a rebel! The Lord in his mercy look upon me and enable me to support myself under this most grievous calamity. I made haste home, and as soon as I could recollect myself a little, I wrote to my Lord Middleton to obtain leave for me to throw myself at the King's feet.

The King expressed sympathy, and said he pitied Clarendon with all his heart. Two weeks later Clarendon himself was heading westward to meet William; not to join him, but in the hope of negotiating a compromise between his brother-in-law, James, and his nephew, William. He was politically out of his depth, however, and James's flight in December put an end to his plans for reconciliation. He protested vehemently in Parliament against the settlement of the crown on William and Mary, and refused to swear an oath of allegiance. Without any hope of office he was advised to go abroad, but instead retired to Cornbury.

He was there for most of the following year, and his diary gives a unique picture of daily life at Cornbury – riding in the park, seeing his neighbours and involving himself with local matters. But politics could not be forgotten, as even at the local level those who refused allegiance to William, the non-jurors, were removed from office.

> March 26. Tuesday. In the morning I rode into the forest. Mr Warren, one of the regarders, dined with me. He came to speak to me of some disorders which had been lately committed in the forest; which I told him I would consider of; and get him, and Sir Littleton Osbaldeston, and some other of the regarders together, before I went out of the country. In the afternoon I went to Langley and Leafield, to settle some concerns I had there. [This must have been one of the last gatherings of regarders, as after the Revolution even these vestiges of Forest Law disappeared.]
>
> March 27. Wednesday. The weather was so bad I could not stir out all day.

March 28. Thursday. I stayed all day at home. In the evening Mr. Mayott came to me from the race at Chipping Norton. [Robert Mayott of Fawler was a close friend.]

March 29. Good Friday. I went to Charlbury to church. There was a lieutenant and serjeant beating up for men for my Lord Drogheda, for the service of Ireland: they got but one man here. Mr. Cole the minister supped with me. [Lord Drogheda was gathering troops to fight King James in Ireland; his lack of success in Charlbury must have pleased Clarendon.]

March 30. Saturday. Sir Littleton, Mr. Cary, and Mr. Warren dined with me. I had the keepers with me too; and I settled things with Mr. Warren for remedying the abuses in the forest.

April 1. Monday. In the afternoon Sir William Walter [of Sarsden] came to see me: he told me he expected to be removed from being Sheriff: that he found it was ill-taken he was not at the proclaiming of the King and Queen at Oxford.

June 11. In the afternoon I perfected the purchase of the several fields on the further side of the meadows, at the foot of the new bridge: for which I paid £100.

July 19. The letters today brought me news of my son's regiment being taken from him, and given to his lieutenant-colonel; for which I cannot be concerned. God grant it may make my son reflect, as he ought to do, on the abominable action he committed in deserting the King; which will be a stain in his life, and will stick heavy at my heart as long as I live.

August 11. Sunday. In the morning I went to church at Charlbury, where a stranger officiated, Mr. Cole not having taken the oaths...in the afternoon Colonel Heyling came to see me. He told me he was in the commission of the peace; but that he had not taken the oaths, and was resolved not to take them.

William Cole, the Vicar of Charlbury, may have lost his benefice for refusing the oath, but Clarendon made him his private chaplain at Cornbury and he lived in Charlbury until his death in 1734. Many parishioners continued to treat him as the rightful vicar, and on his death transferred their allegiance to his assistant at Cornbury, John Arrowsmith.

August 23. Friday. In the afternoon I went to Mr. Mayott's: we rode together in the fields, and had a little course with a greyhound.

August 27. Tuesday. I stirred not out of the house all day; only in the evening my wife and I went about the park in the calash.

Sept. 2. Monday. In the morning Mr. London arrived, but went away again in the evening. I got him to set out the ground for planting above the spring, where the seat is, and to lay out the walks by the ponds.

This was George London, superintendent of the royal gardens and the best-known garden designer of the time. He collaborated with Evelyn and was often employed by Wren. Presumably he visited Cornbury on several occasions. The work referred to here may have been in an area by the 'Iron Spring' later known as the Wilderness, or further down the Newell stream towards Southill.

Sept. 9. Monday. In the evening we rode into the forest to take the air. The masons began to work today at the wall upon the terrace walk between the new building and the stable, and promised it should be finished in a month's time.

Sept. 14. Saturday. Being holy-rood day, in the morning my brother and I went a hunting in the forest; which I am sure I had not done at least these fifteen years: we killed one deer, and so went home to dinner. In the afternoon we all took the air in the forest.

Sept. 25. Wednesday. The elms in the park were begun to be pruned.

Oct. 2. Wednesday. My brother and his children left us: I have not a long while enjoyed so much comfort in the company of my near relations. They are fine children, God Almighty bless them; and he is a most kind brother; as in other things, so especially in affording me so much of his company at this time in my present melancholy circumstances. God only knows whether I shall ever enjoy so much pleasant society again; and I ought not to set my heart upon it.

Nov. 3. Sunday. Being cold raw weather we did not go to church, but had prayers at home.

Dec. 28. Saturday. I went into the park and set out the new work by the spring, and made the agreement for it.

In the New Year he went to his wife's family home at Swallowfield in Berkshire, but by the spring he was back at Cornbury.

March 27. In the morning I went to Langley, and settled the pulling down of that part of the house which John Day lives in.

April 10. I dined with Mr. James Perrott: there was nobody but the ranger and Mr. Mayott. We had a very great dinner; but I could not eat, having indeed been much indisposed ever since my return from Swallowfield. As I came home, I went to see Mrs. Mayott; who gave me a little cordial water, and some Venice treacle, which she advised me to take as I went to bed; as I did.

April 11. I thank God I had a very good night, and found myself much better for the treacle.

April 15. I drew the two uppermost ponds by the warren, and laid them dry to be cleansed: the fish were put into the upper island pond.

But politics could not be forgotten, and created problems that no Venice treacle could cure. James had taken an army to Ireland in an attempt to regain his throne, and Clarendon was corresponding with some of his supporters. As the most eminent of the non-jurors he was a natural object of suspicion, and when these letters fell into the hands of the government, in June 1690, he was arrested and sent to the Tower. The order for his arrest was regretfully given by his niece, Queen Mary.

After the Battle of the Boyne, and the final defeat of James, the atmosphere eased, and on August 15th Clarendon was released, John Evelyn being one of those who stood bail for him. He immediately returned to Cornbury, and was soon distracting himself with the fish-ponds.

August 29. Drew the upper Island Pond, and sent home six large carps: put into the stew twenty large ones, and into the pond by the Warren corner ninety-eight very fair ones. Put into the pond by the dog kennel sixteen young jacks.

Sept. 17. Drew great Newill pond, and put into the pond by the Warren corner two hundred and eighty-three carps. Into the upper Island Pond three hundred and sixty-eight; and in the lower Island Pond five hundred and thirty-two.

From Cornbury he wrote to Evelyn, and referred to the trees which had been planted according to Evelyn's advice twenty-six years before:

My stay in town was so short, after my release, that I had not an opportunity of thanking you for your great kindness; and therefore I

One of the lakes at Cornbury (c.1920).

endeavour to do it this way, and beg you to believe that I will always remember and acknowledge it. I should take it for a very great favour, if you would take a journey hither. The flying coach goes to Oxford in a day, all this month, and if you will let me know when you will be there, I will meet you with my coach. The plantation pretends to be one of your eldest children, and therefore claims some sort of your care; it was designed by yourself, and the performance had once the approbation of your view. I have since, by little and little, and I may say not unsuccessfully, so far finished the whole, that I thank God I taste the benefit as well as the pleasure of the work; and your presence would now give a blessing to all. Let me, therefore, beg you to throw away a little of your precious time upon your friends at a place where I hope you believe you shall be most really welcome.

For whatever reason, Evelyn did not come, and a month later Clarendon wrote again:

I am very sorry your occasions would not permit you to allow us the favour of your company. I verily believe you would have been pleased (if I may say so of myself) to have seen so prosperous a plantation as this is, made and carried on by your instructions; indeed, I have many things to brag of, and some which are not ordinary; and I bless

God I can please myself perfectly well with the entertainments the place affords me.

Evelyn, however, was not his only correspondent. He was still writing to King James, and in January 1691 he was back in the Tower, this time for six months. On July 4th he was released and was allowed to retire to Cornbury. The following year he was released from bail, and by 1695 William had forgiven him sufficiently to pay him a visit at Cornbury.

By now Clarendon's problems were not only political but financial. His continued refusal of allegiance to William deprived him of public office and its rewards, and he had never been good at dealing with his own affairs. Bishop Burnet wrote of him:

> The Earl of Clarendon is a man naturally sincere, except in the payment of his debts, in which he has a peculiar art, upon his breaking of his promise, which he does very often, to have a plausible excuse and a new promise ever ready at hand, in which he has run longer than one could think possible. He is a friendly and good-natured man.

In 1678 he had mortgaged Cornbury and Langley Manor; then in 1683 he sold Clarendon House in London to Sir Henry Bond, who promptly demolished it. His father's collection of pictures was moved to Cornbury, and many of them were damaged en route. Trees were cut down in the Park, and much of the Park itself put under the plough, while other areas were used for grazing. Finally, in 1694, the promises ran out and the bailiffs moved in. His father's library and pictures were seized and put up for sale, though many were bought back by his brother Laurence. Laurence, loyal to his elder brother and fond of him as he was, was now getting increasingly anxious. In 1685 he had lent him £5000 for which he had no security or interest, and was concerned about the burden of debt his children would inherit if he died. So he began to negotiate with Clarendon about buying all his Oxfordshire estates, Cornbury itself, and the manor of Witney.

Clarendon was reluctant for fear of losing face: as Laurence wrote

> He had a certain kind of fondness to remain in appearance the master of Cornbury; but on the promise that the sale of Cornbury should be entirely a secret, that he should appear to be still the master of it, and that if I should act anything there, in making improvements in the

park or otherwise, it should be so managed that it should look as if done by his direction and appointment, he consented to make an absolute sale.

So the sale was kept secret, and exactly when it took place is not clear. But by 1697 it appears to have been completed, since Laurence's Will dated on July 27th refers to Witney and Cornbury 'which my dear brother's circumstances indispensably obliged him to part with, and mine very hardly permitted me to comply with.' Laurence paid £9810 for lands in Witney, and £7500 for Cornbury itself, including the picture collection, and all the first Earl of Clarendon's papers. The latter remained at Cornbury for many years, in the custody of the non-juror ex-vicar of Charlbury, William Cole, now Librarian and Chaplain at Cornbury.

For the rest of his life Clarendon remained loyal to the exiled King whose religion he so disliked. When Queen Anne succeeded in 1702 he went to St. James' Palace, and asked for 'admittance to his niece'. The Queen sent word that 'if he would qualify himself to enter her presence by taking the oath of loyalty, she would be very glad to see him.' 'No,' he replied, 'I am come to talk to my niece; I shall take no other oath than I have taken already.' The Queen refused to see him, though she granted him a pension of £1500 a year, and he remained a non-juror until his death, which took place in October 1709. Like his father, he was buried in Westminster Abbey.

When he died, his son and heir, Lord Cornbury, was lying in a debtor's prison in New York. The historical reputation of Edward Hyde, Viscount Cornbury and now 3rd Earl of Clarendon, could hardly be worse. Macaulay in his *History* wrote of him that 'his conduct through life was a blot upon his name, and brought down upon him the scorn and reproach of two hemispheres.' Even though he had been the first to go over to William in 1688, the latter never trusted him, and his regiment was taken from him. By 1698 his financial distress was such that the King ordered £10 per week to be paid to him for subsistence, every Monday morning. But when his cousin Anne succeeded in 1702 she appointed him Governor of the colonies of New York and New Jersey. In American mythology Lord Cornbury has become the epitome of corrupt and irresponsible colonial rule. Accused of embezzlement and religious persecution, his reputation was not enhanced by the tale that on the Queen's Birthday he received the official world of Albany wearing female dress, the better to represent Her Majesty. He was also said to have had his portrait painted in this costume. Complaints about him led to his recall in 1708, but as soon as he lost the immunity of his Governorship he was thrown into jail by his New York creditors. He was only released when his father's death made him a peer.

However, a recent book by an American scholar, Patricia Bonomi, has shown how this reputation is based, not on contemporary evidence, but on anti-colonial propaganda of the Revolutionary period, which has been accepted unquestioningly by later writers on both sides of the Atlantic. She demonstrates clearly that he was a competent and respected governor, who was the victim of the scurrilous inventiveness of his political opponents. This is confirmed by events on his return to England in 1710. There is no sign that he was in any kind of disgrace. He was appointed to the Privy Council in 1711, made First Commissioner of the Admiralty in 1712, and in 1713 was granted an annual pension of £2000. Most significantly, when Queen Anne was dying in 1714 she sent him as her Ambassador to the future George I in Hanover. Such a sensitive role would hardly have been granted to the corrupt buffoon of tradition. Anne had chosen him, she wrote to the Elector, not only as her cousin, but because of her knowledge of his ability; she was sure George would soon perceive his merit. He was well received in Hanover, and it was reported that 'he is very much caressed by the whole court.' After George's accession the Whigs became dominant, but he remained a leading figure among the Tory Lords. He died in 1723, and joined his forbears in the Abbey. His last years must have been unhappy ones. Cornbury Park had gone, and he had been forced to sell his mother's estate of Swallowfield in 1719. His wife had died in New York, and all his children had predeceased him. His earldom now passed to his cousin, who was already Earl of Rochester. At least he did not know how his enemies would succeed in destroying his reputation for nearly three centuries.

Laurence Hyde, into whose hands Cornbury passed in the late 1690s, was born in 1641. Renowned for his uncontrollable temper and addiction to the bottle, he was nevertheless one of the major political personalities of his day. With similar views to his brother, he was a man of much greater political ability, and held several major offices during the reign of Charles II. In Dryden's poem *Absalom and Achitophel* he appears as Hushai:

Hushai, the friend of David in distress,
In public storms of manly steadfastness;
By foreign treaties he informed his youth,
And joined experience to his native truth.

It was he who negotiated the secret treaty with France in 1681, by which the King received a subsidy from Louis XIV and avoided dependence on Parliament. That autumn he was rewarded with the Earldom of Rochester.

After James II's accession he kept his office as Lord High Treasurer, but was dismissed in 1687. In 1688, like his brother, he opposed the offer of the throne to William; but unlike Clarendon, he eventually accepted the new political reality and took the oath of allegiance to the new monarchs. After a few years he was readmitted to the Privy Council, gained a considerable influence over his niece Mary II, and established himself as head of the High Church (Tory) party. Towards the end of William's reign he became Lord-Lieutenant of Ireland, a post in which he remained until 1703.

Although Rochester's acquisition of Cornbury was secret, Clarendon's dire financial state must have been widely known, and in 1700 the Duke of Shrewsbury, who was renting Heythrop House nearby, showed interest in renting or buying Cornbury. Some surviving letters that passed between the Duke and Rochester tell us something about the state of Cornbury at this time, and give an interesting glimpse of courteous aristocratic bargaining.

Shrewsbury to Rochester: (February 3rd 1699/1700)

The condition of my health requiring me to be almost always in the country, the wretchedness of the house I am now in [Heythrop], and my other house in Worcestershire being lately in part burned down, had put me upon fresh thoughts of building, for want of a decent place to live in; but since my Lord Clarendon has no thoughts of selling Cornbury, if he were disposed to let it for any term, I would rather choose to be his tenant, than enter upon building, which is what I very much dread, and very little understand. I know the house and stables suffer for want of being lived in, and the maintaining them and the gardens are a considerable expense, so that upon account of good husbandry I am sure it were advisable to admit a tenant...

Rochester to Shrewsbury: (February 9th 1699/1700)

This particular of letting your Grace into Cornbury as a tenant must needs seem so reasonable to you, that I am very much concerned there should be any difficulties in it...The park hath been turned almost into a farm, not let, but part of it ploughed; a good deal of wood cut and carried off, that more may be ploughed, part already laid down with cinquefoil; which was only for a pattern some years ago, to see how that husbandry would suit the ground; and by that we have been encouraged to go on with the greater quantities; another part of the park turned to grazing and every part to the best advantage; and it hath been turned to above £300 profit for one year, and gives hopes of increasing considerably.

The incumbrances that lie upon that estate, and in some measure upon myself, that am engaged in the management of it, having made it necessary to seek out all manner of improvements upon it: and how this can be accommodated with the pleasure your Grace would propose to have of the park in your living there, I confess I cannot see.

Shrewsbury to Rochester: (February 12th 1699/1700)

I agree the difficulties your Lordship proposes are very just, and would be insurmountable, if I pretended to take the whole Park at Cornbury, and to have deer in it, as formerly has been; but my chief aim being only the house, and that part of the lands next the house being at present grazed, and not let, I shall be satisfied with what you do not design to plough, which I suppose is that which lies under the gardens, between them and the ponds, and between the stable and Charlbury. If there be any person here in the country you entrust with the management of the estate, and thought fit to direct him to discourse with me about it, it is possible we might agree to offer something which might not be unacceptable; and if the profits of the estate, by what I will give, will answer to what your Lordship expects by husbandry, I suppose you would think it an advantage to the place, if less of the land (especially of that near the house) were ploughed. I have heard there are advantages of wood and other particulars, which arise from the command of the forest, which, if I should live there, would be such a convenience to me, that I would either rent that, or not, as should be most agreeable to your Lordship.

Rochester agreed that Actaeon Kew, the estate manager, should discuss the matter with Shrewsbury – 'He is but a plain man, but I think he is honest,

Thorns in Cornbury Park (c. 1910).

and I believe will not tell you a lie.' The meeting took place, and Shrewsbury seemed happy with what he learned.

Shrewsbury to Rochester: (March 1st 1699/1700)

We agreed that in case I became tenant to the house, I must necessarily rent that part of the Park which is not broken up, and which lies between the house and the ponds; he told me whereabouts he thought the value of that piece of ground was, viz. about eight score pounds a year. I do not doubt but the bargain will be pretty hard, but however, if we can agree upon all other points, I shall not differ for that... I should likewise wish that all or most of the furniture might remain: most of it is not very good, and will hardly be worth removing, but will be of great convenience to me if I may have the use of it.

I am much ashamed to reflect how much trouble I have given your Lordship upon this affair, but if you saw in what a place I live, you would pity and excuse the importunity.

Rochester to Shrewsbury: (March 7th 1699/1700)

It will be a difficult matter for me to set a price for the letting of the house at Cornbury, since your Grace is pleased to say it would be a pretty hard bargain to pay eight score pounds a year for that part of the Park you propose to take along with the house, which I suppose Act. Kew could demonstrate it had made last year, and in all probability was to make more this; but I hope I shall show my duty to your Grace as much by leaving it to yourself to say what your own price shall be.

The furniture, such as it is, which indeed is very bad for your Grace, shall be left at your service, except the linen and pewter, which would quickly be worn out. There may be several other particulars necessary to be adjusted, which since you are pleased to offer it, I should wish may be determined here by such person as you shall be pleased to send to me; in which I hope I shall not be difficult or unreasonable. The library you will allow to be locked up, for books may easily be lost or mislaid.

And now my Lord I must acquaint your Grace what nobody in the country knows yet, and I desire may not; that I have finished the bargain with my brother that I have been some time about, and so the house and Park and all belonging to it is in my hands.

It is not the less at your service, and if I shall find it reasonable for me to part with it, I shall ever be desirous to make an offer of it to your Grace rather than any other body.

It looks as if a bargain might have been struck, since Rochester would never live at Cornbury himself. (He lived at Petersham House in Richmond Park, where he held the Rangership) But when Shrewsbury learned that the estate was now Rochester's, he lost interest. It seems that his real aim was purchase rather than renting. A few years later he bought the Heythrop Estate, and built a new house for himself there.

It was shortly after the purchase of Cornbury that Clarendon and Rochester arranged the publication of their father's *History of the Rebellion*, his narrative account of the Civil War. It was published at Oxford in 1702-4, and the profits were used to provide a building for the University Press, now known as the Clarendon Building, which was erected in 1713.

In 1710 Rochester's political fortunes seemed to have revived with those of the Tory party, and he became Lord President of the Council. But on

May 2nd 1711 he suddenly died at his house in London. On hearing of his death Louis XIV commented, 'Rochester dead? Then there is not a man of probity and counsel equal to him left in the world!' He was succeeded by his son Henry, who became 2nd Earl of Rochester and also, after the death of his cousin in 1723, 4th Earl of Clarendon. He had been born in 1672, and had been M.P. for Launceston since 1692. He was noted for his good looks, and when he married Jane Leveson-Gower they were described as 'the finest couple ever seen'; he appears to have had little other distinction, however, and the only public office he held was that of High Steward of Oxford University. His wife was a notable hostess, described by Jonathan Swift as 'for long my principal goddess'. Like his father he lived at Petersham House in Richmond Park, but retained sufficient connection with Oxfordshire to give a silver flagon and basin to Charlbury Church in 1716. In 1721 his house at Richmond was burned down, and presumably he then moved to Cornbury.

The next generation of the Hydes, however, made a greater impact on their world. Both daughters were noted beauties and wits; and the son, the last man to bear the title of Viscount Cornbury, had connections with many of the literary and political figures of the day, and was widely admired as a man of principle, intelligence and courtesy. He was born in 1710, and became M.P. for Oxford University in 1732. He was initially a committed supporter of the Jacobite cause, and in 1731, while on the Grand Tour, he met the Chevalier de St.George, the 'Old Pretender', in Rome. He was representing a group of Tory nobles, who were plotting the restoration of the Stuarts; and two years later he went to Paris to tell the French government about their plans for a rising, and to ask for military assistance. But the French failed to deliver, and in 1735 Cornbury broke off his connection with the Stuarts. Then for a while he was numbered among the 'Young Patriot' opposition to the Whig premier Sir Robert Walpole, which also included William Pitt; but by 1740 he was moving closer to the government, and spoke in their support during the 1745 Jacobite rising. His name does not appear in the list of supporters that the Jacobites compiled, and the legend that Jacobite gentry gathered at Cornbury in 1745 is unlikely to be true.

However, in 1746 he visited Paris and met Prince Charles Edward for the first time; bowled over by the Prince's charm his old loyalties reasserted

Henry Hyde, Viscount Cornbury, Lord Hyde of Hindon. From a portrait by Van Loo.

themselves and, he says, he 'committed twenty extravagancies' in the Prince's company. This makes the other legend, of Charles's visit to Cornbury in 1750, more probable. In September of that year the Young Pretender was in London incognito, when he inspected the defences of the Tower of London, and he may well have visited Oxfordshire to meet his many supporters there. It is said that the local barber, Mr. Banbury, was summoned to Cornbury in 1750 to shave a strange gentleman and dress his wig. From the deference shown to the stranger, and an incautious word dropped by Lord Cornbury, Banbury realised who it was he had just shaved, and the word soon spread.

By now, however, Cornbury's political career was over. Too honest for the corrupt world of Hanoverian politics, and suffering from continual ill-health, by 1748 he had despaired of being able to do any good and petitioned the King to be allowed to go abroad. He considered, he wrote, 'party division and distinction the greatest national misfortune', yet to remain in Parliament as an independent was futile: 'I knew the inefficiency and had long felt the difficulty of standing single and unconnected in that assembly.' In 1750 he resigned his seat and moved to the Lords as Lord Hyde of Hindon.

In 1735, as he was renouncing Jacobitism, he took over responsibility for running the family estates. His father, the Earl of Clarendon and Rochester, made little mark on history, but had managed to run up a considerable debt, and made a formal agreement to hand everything over to his son at a peppercorn rent, in return for an allowance of £2000 a year.[1] Cornbury himself would take £500 a year, and the rest of the estate income would be used to pay off the Earl's debts. This must have been put into immediate effect, since within a few years there were funds available for considerable alterations to both House and Park: a clause in the agreement allows Lord Cornbury to use any profits from felling trees in the Park for 'making Plantations or any other Ornaments or Conveniences in the said Park and for repairing or adorning the Capital Messuage there.'

Over the next few years the House was renovated and the gardens redesigned; one of the advisers for the latter was the poet Alexander Pope, who was a close friend. When in London Pope would stay at Cornbury's house, and was frequently summoned to Cornbury Park to advise. In 1739 he wrote to his friend Fortescue from Rousham:

> My Lord Cornbury came hither to General Dormer's, and insists so urgently, that he did so, purely to get me to Cornbury for some days (where I formerly made, and am to make, some alterations) that I can't refuse it.

Alexander Pope

Pope was there again in 1743; the nature of his advice is unknown, but there was still at the beginning of the twentieth century a spot in the Wilderness, overlooking the ponds, covered with ancient yew-trees, known as Pope's Mount. Pope's admiration for Lord Cornbury is expressed in these lines from *Imitations of Horace Epistle I vi*:

> Would ye be blessed? Despise low joys, low gains;
>
> Disdain whatever Cornbury disdains;
>
> Be virtuous, and be happy for your pains. (ll. 60-62)

Cornbury's other literary connections include James Thomson, who refers to him in *The Seasons* as 'polished Cornbury' ('Summer', l. 1420), John Gay, at whose funeral he was a pallbearer, and Horace Walpole. Visitors to Cornbury Park during these years also included the politician and philosopher Lord Bolingbroke, William Pitt, the future Prime Minister, and the future Chief Justice Lord Mansfield. The most detailed description of the now greatly improved House and gardens comes from the letters of Mary Granville, Mrs Delany, written in 1743. Married to the Dean of Down, and a distant relative of Lord Cornbury, she was also a friend and correspondent of Swift, and in later life a friend of the novelist Fanny Burney. Having spent the night at Burford, she and the Dean

> ...set forward for Cornbury, and sent a messenger forward to ask leave to go through the Park, and to say if my Lord C. was alone we would breakfast with him: he sent back an invitation to us to dine as well as breakfast, and entertained us with showing us his house, pictures and park, which, indeed, are all as well worth seeing as anything in England, especially when he is there to do the honours. The house has no regular front; it is unfinished, but newly fitted up with great elegance, and contains a number of very fine rooms; the lower apartment is just finished, and is the prettiest thing I ever saw... His park lies finely to the house and is most charming, and kept as nice as a garden, and a gravel path quite round it, that you may walk in any weather. The ground lies most advantageously, and is planted with great skill and great variety of fine trees, some thick wood, some clumps; in short, nature and art have done their best to make it beautiful... I had almost forgot to speak particularly of the pictures: they are excessively fine, most of them Vandykes, whole lengths, and a vast number of them. Either the painter or the persons painted had more gracefulness than the modern nobility, for they *all* look like *valet-de-chambres* compared to their ancestors. As Lord Cornbury led me to the coach, he said he was 'obliged to me that he now belonged to Dr. Delaney, and that he had a right to claim his friendship and acquaintance.'

The remark that Cornbury had no regular front and was unfinished probably refers to the fact that the entrance was not in either of the main fronts, but in an inner courtyard and had no porch. In 1746 Mrs Delany was back for a longer visit, and her letter not only describes the house and park, but gives a good impression of a Georgian house-party:

We left Chip. at four, and got to Cornbury by half an hour after five, where we were expected, and immediately conveyed into the apartment allotted for us – which is so neat and so elegant that I never saw anything equal to it. It consists of two large rooms and a bedchamber: the first room is hung with flowered paper of a grotesque pattern, the colours lively and the patterns bold and handsome (that is the Dean's dressing room); the next room is hung with the finest Indian paper of flowers and *all sorts of birds* (that is my dressing room); the ceilings are all ornamented in the Indian taste, the frames of the glass and all the finishing of the room are well-suited; the bedchamber is also hung with Indian paper on a gold ground, and the bed is *Indian work* of silks and gold on a white satin; the windows look into the park, which is kept like the finest garden, and is a Paradise. The great apartment above-stairs is very fine: the room we sit in after dinner is 48 foot long and two and twenty wide; the walls are covered with whole lengths of Vandyke, and so are two large rooms besides that belong to the Duchess of Queensbury's apartment. [The Duchess of Queensbury was Cornbury's sister.] I have not time to describe the house more minutely, but upon the whole I think the house *the most comfortable and pleasant fine house* I ever saw, for it is not only magnificent and elegant, but *convenient* and *rational*; it resembles its master, and is both strong and genteel, nothing can be more agreeable than his behaviour.

Lord Cornbury looks thin and dejected, but strives to exert himself for the entertainment of his company. We meet at breakfast between nine and ten, which lasts near two hours intermixed with conversations; when over, the coach is ready for Dr Delany and me to tour in the park, and to see my lord's improvements; the rest of the company ride. I never saw any spot of ground more beautiful than the park. I have taken a sketch of one part, which was originally a stone quarry, and is now improved into the wildest, prettiest place

The beech avenue in Cornbury Park.

you can imagine – winding walks, mounts covered with all sorts of trees and flowering shrubs, rocks covered with moss, hollows filled with bushes intermixed with rocks, rural seats and sheds; and in the valley beneath a river winds and accomplishes the beauty. We return home at two and spruce out; dinner at half an hour after two; the afternoon – coffee, sauntering, conversation comes on, and tea; my drawings produced, many civilities are uttered, and the whole ends with a pool at commerce, which brings us to our hour of supper; and we go to our separate apartments at eleven.

Mrs. Delany tells us that the house had been 'newly fitted up' in 1743, and it is likely that the 'Indian' decorations she describes were actually in the Chinese style, which was then coming into fashion. The 'apartment' assigned to the Delanys was probably on the ground floor of the Clarendon wing.

In 1749 Lord Cornbury took over full legal possession of the family estates from his father, who was now in his seventies. He soon decided that it was beyond his capacity to maintain Cornbury, however, and his giving up his political career and moving abroad must have confirmed him in his decision that Cornbury had to be sacrificed. So, in 1751, the whole estate was sold to his neighbour, Charles Spencer, the third Duke of Marlborough. It must have been painful, but he was supported by his father, who wrote kindly and generously: 'I wish Cornbury House could have been kept for you to enjoy, but as matters were I think you have taken a prudent course, and am glad you have got through it. It is a fine and pleasant thing to be out of debt; but as I told you before, you may comfort yourself with the thought that it has not been your fault.'

At one time it seemed that the famous collection of pictures would also have to go. These were the ones collected by the first Earl of Clarendon for his house in London, and had been praised by Evelyn, envied by Pepys, and admired by Horace Walpole. According to the inventory prepared in 1751 in connection with the sale of the estate, there were 242 pictures in all. Most of them were portraits, and included 22 Vandykes, 9 Lelys, and others by Kneller, Wissing, Cornelius Jansen and Honthorst.

For a while, however, they remained at Cornbury with the Duke of Marlborough's permission, labelled and sealed with the Hyde seal. They were intended as an heirloom for the Hydes, but in 1763 a family dispute led to their being divided between the families of the 4th Lord Clarendon's two daughters, and they were removed from Cornbury. Half went to The Grove at Watford, the home of Thomas Villiers, the son-in-law of Clarendon's eldest daughter, who would later, in 1776, be created Earl of Clarendon. The rest went to the Duchess of Queensbury's house in Amesbury, from where they were removed to Bothwell and later dispersed.

However painful the sale of Cornbury it was also a relief, as can be seen in a letter from Lord Cornbury to an old friend, Miss Anne Pitt:

Though you will have heard in general that my affairs at last are ended, I owe to you, Madam, to tell you myself that they are ended to my entire satisfaction. By which you may be sure they are entirely ended. My health is much mended. I may probably never have more health and liberty than I at present enjoy, and I am therefore tempted to gratify an inclination which I have long had to see the southern provinces of France.

But he was not to enjoy for long this new-found release from anxiety. He moved to Paris, where he rented a house. According to Henry Conway, in a letter to Horace Walpole:

> His house is pretty; he has laid out a good deal of money on it, lives a good deal among the French, by whom he's very well received, and enters into all the gaiety of a Paris life.

In 1753, however, he was killed by falling from his horse; and eight months later his father died, and with him all the family titles. Everyone lamented Cornbury's death; according to Mrs Delany, 'I think his parting with Cornbury was a presage that he was not long to enjoy it. Of all the young men of quality with whom I have been acquainted he was the prime.' 'He had,' wrote Horace Walpole,

> one of the best hearts that ever warmed a human breast. He was upright, calm, and steady. His virtues were of the gentlest complexion, yet of the firmest texture. Vice could not bend him, nor party warp him; even his own talents could not mislead him. Though a master of eloquence, he preferred justice and the love of his country to all the applause which the violence of the times in which he lived was so prodigal of bestowing on orators who distinguished themselves in any faction; but the tinsel of popularity, and the intrinsic of corruption, were equally his contempt. He spoke, nor wrote, nor acted, for fame. Goodness was the object and end of all his actions.

In his Will, he left the manuscripts of his great-grandfather, Lord Chancellor Clarendon, to the University of Oxford, with a direction that the University Press should publish whatever was felt appropriate, and that any profits should be used to establish a school 'for riding and other useful exercises'. The Lord Chancellor had seen riding as an important part of a gentleman's education. It was many years before there were any significant profits, but by 1868 about £12,000 had accumulated in the 'Cornbury Fund'. It was then used to build laboratories and lecture-rooms for the Professor of Experimental Philosophy – the Clarendon Laboratory.

Note

1 Draft Agreement in Oxfordshire County Archive, Misc.Lem. I/i BRA273

🐌 7

The End of the Forest

After 1688 all semblance of the traditional management of the Royal Forests disappeared. The last Forest Eyre in southern England had been held in Hampshire in 1672, though the office of Justice in Eyre still existed as a sinecure. (Its holder received three bucks a year from Wychwood.) Other Forest Offices became, in the words of a late eighteenth-century report, 'Marks of Favour and Distinction bestowed upon Gentlemen of Consideration in the Neighbourhood rather than Appointments of Real Use or Responsibility.' Such central responsibility as existed was exercised by the Surveyor-General of Woods and Forests, who saw to repairs to property, royal gifts to subjects, and the felling of trees for the Navy. Surveyors-General cannot have troubled Wychwood much – not a single tree was felled there for the Navy between 1700 and 1786.

Repairs were another matter, as Gentlemen of Consideration holding Forest Offices wanted houses in decent condition. In 1734 we catch a glimpse of Wychwood's Forest Officers in action. The Acting Ranger, (Baptist Leveson Gower), the Verderers, (Robert Lee and Robert B. Jenkinson) and the Keepers (Charles Jenkinson, John Blackstone, Stephen Bruce, William Short) petitioned the Lords of the Treasury, saying that the lodges and other premises at Wychwood Forest were in such a ruinous condition that they were neither safe nor fit for His Majesty's said officers to reside and do their duty in.

The petition led to a report the following year from the Surveyor-General. He stated that:

Burford Lawn Lodge wanted a thorough repair, stables, sheds and rails
£150

Potter's Hill Lodge, William Short, keeper, wanted tiling, paving, thatching, paling, etc.
£50

Moated Lodge, Mr. John Blackstone, keeper, wanted tiling, paling,
and railing, etc.   £100
Ranger's Lodge, and premises, the Honourable Baptist Leveson Gower,
keeper, were in so bad a repair that it could not be done with any good
husbandry, but must be rebuilt, which would cost   £300

To remedy this the Surveyor-General was ordered to cut down 'so many
dotard and decayed trees, as also hornbeams, thorns etc., as by the sale
thereof and of the lops, tops and offal wood of the same' should be sufficient to raise £600.

Both verderers were, as they always had been, local gentry: the Lees
were of Ditchley, the Jenkinsons of Walcot. Leveson Gower was Lady
Clarendon's cousin. Charles Jenkinson may well have occupied Burford
Lawn Lodge. As South Lawn Lodge it was in later years, together with
Ranger's Lodge, definitely a gentleman's residence, while the other lodges,
and their keepers, were altogether humbler.

The Rangership of Wychwood, with all its perquisites, was valued at
£10,000, and in 1751 it passed to the third Duke of Marlborough, when
he bought Cornbury and the other Hyde lands in Oxfordshire for the
overall sum of £61,000. Cornbury was now renamed 'Blandford Park', and
must have been intended as a home for the heir to the dukedom, the
Marquess of Blandford. However, the current heir was still a boy, and was
only 19 when he became the 4th Duke of Marlborough in 1758, on the
early death of his father.

So it is likely that Cornbury House was unoccupied for many years, but
from about 1770 it was used regularly by the 5th Duke of Beaufort. He and
his son, the 6th Duke, hunted the area for over 60 years, as well as the land
around the Duke's home at Badminton. Each year in mid-September the
whole household would ride from Badminton to Cornbury, return to
Badminton at Christmas, and then back to Cornbury in February for the rest
of the season. Master and hounds, huntsman and whippers-in, manservants
and maidservants, all took to the road, and the journey was no easy one.

Everybody that could be got on a horse had to ride one of the
hunters, the footmen, even some of the maidservants. They arrived
in a state of stiffness, soreness and exhaustion, especially the French
cook, who was no lover of horses, after riding between forty and fifty

The Heythrop Hunt at Cornbury, early twentieth century.

miles. They were able to ride on grass all the way and wagons containing luggage and other family impedimenta followed as best they could.

The reason for all this dislocation was that Wychwood had more foxes than Badminton; the Forest itself carried a good scent, and was an excellent place for training hounds. It was there, and in the woodland around Ditchley, that the hunting would begin in early autumn. Kennels were built for the hounds near Buckleap Coppice, on the site of kennels built long before for the Earl of Danby. About the end of the century the Duke moved his quarters to Heythrop; but when in 1831 Heythrop House was destroyed by fire he returned to Wychwood, this time to Ranger's Lodge. In 1835, shortly before his death, the Duke retired from the Mastership, and the hunt changed its name from the Beaufort to the Heythrop Hunt. The kennels were later replaced by cottages for estate workers.

During their 60-year association with the area the Beauforts put down roots that extended beyond hunting. The 6th Duchess in particular, known locally as 'The Good Duchess', involved herself in local charities. She set up a training workshop for 20 girls, where they were taught to prepare straws for hat-making, and soon became able to earn themselves a good living. She and the Duke became patrons of the British School opened in

Charlbury in 1816. The Duchess also struck up an unusual friendship with the Quaker weaver William Jones, who addressed her democratically as 'neighbour Buffet', and would 'visit her to edification' in her London home.

The Joint Master of the new Heythrop Hunt was Lord Churchill of Whichwood, who was now owner of Cornbury and Ranger of the Forest. As Lord Francis Spencer, the favoured younger son of the 4th Duke of Marlborough, he had moved into Cornbury on his marriage in 1801 to Lady Frances Fitzroy, daughter of the Duke of Grafton, and probably became Ranger of Wychwood at the same time. They brought up a large family, of eight sons and four daughters, and he inherited Cornbury on his Father's death in 1817. In 1801 his Father had arranged for him to become M.P. for Oxfordshire: 'He has a great desire to be in Parliament, and we shall wish him to stand somewhere, where there is no chance of any contest,' wrote the Duke. Lord Francis may have wished to be in Parliament, but he was hardly a keen Parliamentarian: he gave his maiden speech reluctantly in 1806, and is not known to have spoken again. His Father had higher ambitions for him: he had given his son Cornbury, the Duke wrote to the Prince Regent, to enable him to support the dignity of a peerage. He hoped for a Viscountcy but finally settled for a Barony, and in 1815 Lord Francis became the first Lord Churchill of Whichwood. [This is the spelling commonly used in the nineteenth century; Watney gives a list of no fewer than 71 variant spellings found in documents from the 9th to the 16th centuries.]

'Blandford Park' was never occupied by a Lord Blandford; Lord Francis's elder brother had married without his father's permission, and the two were not on speaking terms. After inheriting the estate, Lord Churchill took to heading his letters from 'Whichwood Park', but the name did not take on. The names of 'Cornbury' and 'Blandford' were both used until the mid-nineteenth century, when the latter fell into disuse.

In the first decade of the century Lord Francis did much to make the Forest more picturesque, cutting ridings and lights through the woodland, opening up new vistas. The Tower Light, running from the Forest across the Park, aligned on Charlbury Church Tower, and the Grand Vista, a wide sweep of grass running from the edge of the Park to Newell Plain and beyond, date from this time, and appear on an Estate Map of 1815. Neither is marked on the Davis map of 1792. The Ordnance Survey map of 1833

View of Cornbury in 1826. From a drawing by John Buckler.

also shows the Hazelwood Light running straight from Ranger's Lodge to Buckleap Copse. These are all visible on maps today, but a further light of 1833, running WSW from Newell Plain to Fairspear, has largely disappeared. The 1833 map also shows that the Newell stream had been landscaped, with the ponds becoming larger and fewer. Finally, Lord Francis employed the architect Henry Hakewill, the excavator of the Roman Villa at North Leigh, to make some alterations to the House, though this work is not now traceable.

Lord Francis's best-known public activity was with the Oxfordshire Yeomanry. Founded in 1798, it was reconstituted and enlarged in 1802 after the short-lived Peace of Amiens, when Lord Francis formed a new Woodstock Troop. As Captain, he led 80 troopers, mainly local farmers, tradesmen and estate servants, each of whom had to provide his own horse. Like the Home Guard of a later era, the Yeomanry were intended to be the last line of defence against invasion, but the Woodstock Troop were far more splendidly attired, in scarlet uniforms with yellow facings. By 1817 it had become the Woodstock Squadron, with three troops; the following year it was joined by the Wootton Troop, and became the First Oxfordshire Regiment of Yeomanry Cavalry, with Lord Churchill as its Colonel.

The Yeomanry never had to face an invasion; their only action was against the Otmoor rioters in 1832, and it was not a glorious occasion. The people of Otmoor, in protest against enclosure, had pulled down the newly erected stakes and hedges, and the Yeomanry were called out 'in support of the civil power'. They arrested a number of rioters and escorted them to Oxford, where in St Giles a large crowd attacked them with cries of 'unhorse the buggers!' and freed their prisoners. 'The Troopers came home "with all their blushing honours thick upon them," and some who were not used to riding, terribly galled in their seats.' They were more in their element providing a colourful escort on ceremonial occasions, as when the Prince Regent came to Oxford in 1814, with the Tsar and the King of Prussia; or when Queen Adelaide visited in 1835, after which the Regiment was granted the title of The Queen's Own Oxfordshire Yeomanry Cavalry. It was usually referred to, more economically, as Lord Churchill's Regiment.

In 1809 Wychwood Forest was visited by Arthur Young, Secretary to the Board of Agriculture and a strong supporter of enclosure. His condemnation of its condition is well known. In a ride of 16 or 17 miles, he wrote, he did not see a single 'navy oak'; there were quite a number of 60-70 year old trees, which could be useful after another century, but even these were insignificant compared with the extent of the Forest. He concluded that 'there is not the smallest reason to judge...that this Forest will ever be productive of navy timber in the least degree answerable to its extent.'

Vernon Watney adds a sly footnote to this quotation from Young: 'When Young's *View of Agriculture in Oxfordshire* was published, his eyesight had long been failing him, and he was nearly blind.' His inability to see any navy trees in the Forest is not borne out by the record of the felling of such trees at the time he was writing, and it may be that his support of enclosure affected his vision as much as his cataract. For him, enclosure was not just an economic issue, but a moral one, as he explains in round terms:

> The morals of the whole surrounding country demand it imperiously. The vicinity is filled with poachers, deer-stealers, thieves and pilferers of every kind; offences of almost every description abound so much, that the offenders are a terror to all quiet and well-disposed persons; and Oxford gaol would be uninhabited, were it not for this fertile source of crimes.

This may sound excessive, but another writer of the time refers to 'that nest and conservatory of sloth, idleness and misery, which is uniformly to be witnessed in the vicinity of all commons, waste lands and forests.'

The harsh moralism of these judgements is off-putting, but the folklore of the district goes some way to reinforce them. Of the Forest inhabitants it was said that 'they keep themselves to themselves, and queer goings-on there be in the Forest.' The people of Shipton were rough and uncouth, and strangers were stoned as a matter of course. Bull-baiting continued at Field Assarts into the 1850s, though it had been made illegal twenty years earlier, and a potter at Leafield bred bull terriers for the baiting. Leafield, also known as Fieldtown, remote and surrounded by woodland, was a particular object of comment. Its inhabitants were 'said to be different from those of surrounding parishes, and to be dark, small, secretive, boastful and unfriendly... To say of a man that he comes from Fieldtown means he is a wife-beater.' Fieldtowners had a great reputation for fighting, and even in the early twentieth century visiting football teams would complain that playing at Leafield was 'plain murder'.

But what really separated the Forest villages from their neighbours was poverty. After the Poor Law reform of the 1830s they were included in the Chipping Norton Union, and were measurably the poorest in the district. The problem was that the Forest provided only casual labour, in the winter when the coppices were cut and re-enclosed. In the summer the men could find some employment with local farmers at haymaking and harvest, but many of them would tramp 'upards' to London to find work in the hayfields of Paddington or Islington. Those who were able would also perform Morris dances to entertain the Londoners, and could earn up to ten shillings a day from this, more than from their haymaking. This was a long established tradition, and the Leafield Morris Men were renowned; but for most Wychwood men this made for an uncertain life, and did not help the development of stable, prosperous communities. It is not surprising that many of them supplemented their income by poaching and wood-stealing. Life in nineteenth-century Wychwood was far from being Merrie England.

It is clear that during the eighteenth century all semblance of the Crown's control over the Royal Forests had disappeared, and they had become a resource to be plundered by all in the neighbourhood, high and low. When Lord Cornbury in the 1740s needed funds for the renovation of Cornbury House and Park, he raised them by cutting down and selling timber from the Forest. When Admiral Pigott, tenant of Ranger's Lodge in the later eighteenth century, needed firewood, he sent his servants to cut it, without seeing any need to ask permission of anyone. And where Admiral Pigott led, humbler folk followed. They were Arthur Young's 'thieves and pilferers'. People from the surrounding villages came openly into the Forest, and carried off what they could, in wagons or on their backs. They would also 'chip the bodies and saw the master roots of the hollow, pollard and dotard oaks, and other trees there, in order to promote windfalls, which the people of the country commonly seize and convert to their own use.' It was the keepers' duty to prevent them, and occasionally they would catch a few, but it was estimated that only one in twenty were prosecuted. They had been doing it for so long that they had come to see it as their natural right, and very much resented any attempt to stop them.

'Offences against the vert' were indeed as old as the Forest, and so were 'offences against the venison'. Deer poaching was widespread, and there are many local stories of the cunning ways in which the venison was concealed –over the church porch, in the upper part of altar tombs, or within hayricks. Once when keepers raided a cottage a venison pie was hidden in the cradle under a sleeping infant. But according to a recent article by Michael Freeman poaching was also part of an organised game trade. Deer were killed not only for the poacher's own pot but for sale to complaisant butchers in Witney. Many respectable locals benefited from the trade. The Bloxham antiquary Oliver Aplin recalled that

> when my father was living in Charlbury early in the [19th] century it was customary for the inhabitants to buy firewood from the woodmen. The men, when arranging with an old customer to send him a load, would ask, 'Should you like anything in it?' The 'anything' would be a quarter of venison in season.[1]

A farmer would sometimes be told firmly to keep away from one of his barns for a few days; if he did so, he would find a haunch of venison in the straw when he returned. 'Left in my barn in a most onaccountable way,' he would tell his neighbours as he feasted them.

The only poachers we know of are those who were caught, and many of them were young craftsmen, rather than the rootless or unemployed. Some would have been commoners, who knew the Forest and its hiding places well, and would also see the deer as competitors for pasture with their own

Lankeridge Copse in the Forest, c. 1910.

animals. Deer stealing was taken seriously by the courts, and could result
in a sentence of transportation; so it was more likely to lead to violence,
including assaults on the keepers.

Most of the local community, therefore, benefited in one way or another
from the collapse of Forest Law, and were unlikely to be enthusiasts for
reform. Arthur Young's report also shows that a new lobby had appeared
to oppose enclosure:

> In riding over the forest I found many very beautiful scenes, partic-
> ularly where the nut fair is held, a glen by Mr Dacre's lodge, and
> others approaching Blandford Park; there are vales also of the finest
> turf. Several of these scenes want nothing but water, to form most
> pleasing and finished landscapes... and no person can doubt, but that
> to the residents who live on or near it, this fine wide tract of country
> affords many agreeable circumstances which may operate...to
> prevent an enclosure which ought, for a thousand reasons, to take
> place as soon as possible.

In the Age of the Picturesque a growing leisure class enjoyed the landscape delights of the Forest and would be loath to see it changed. But all the time its condition was deteriorating, not only because of the uncontrolled cutting of wood, but from over-pasturing of animals. Agistors had disappeared, though 'marksmen' from villages with common rights were meant to control the entry of livestock on to the common land by branding them with their owner's mark. But this system seems to have collapsed: pigs roamed wild throughout the Forest, and oxen, which had never been allowed there, also came to pasture. As nearby parishes were gradually enclosed, the Forest became what Michael Freeman has called 'an island in a sea of enclosures', and was increasingly sought for its common pasture. Lord Churchill and tenants of local manors claimed the right to pasture as many animals as the land would bear. Meanwhile, many local landholdings were so small, and the villagers so poor, that the common pasture in the Forest had become a matter of survival for them. The local ecology deteriorated, and by the 1840s soil compaction and waterlogging from overgrazing caused cattle and sheep to suffer from Johne's disease (bacterial enteritis), and the better farmers began to keep their animals away. When the Forest was finally enclosed and cleared, the farmland proved much less fertile than expected, and was still showing the effects of overgrazing a century later.

The movement for reform began in the late eighteenth century, when, on the initiative of an energetic Surveyor-General of Woods and Forests, John Robinson, a Parliamentary Commission was appointed to investigate all the Royal Forests. It published seventeen reports between 1787 and 1793, that on Wychwood appearing in 1792. This is a major source of information about the Forest and the life of its inhabitants – for example, about the common rights in the Forest referred to in Chapter 1. The Forest was surveyed, and every coppice, riding, sheepwalk, and piece of open land, measured and named. The trees – oak, ash, beech, sycamore, lime, elm, chestnut – were counted, and their age and condition noted. The deer were counted: there were about 1000, of which 61 bucks and 42 does were killed by official warrant each year. Six of each would be sent to the royal larder, some to various officials, and owners of land in the Purlieu; the keepers got one buck and one doe apiece; but the largest single share, of 23 bucks and 13 does, went to the Duke of Marlborough as Ranger.

The Commissioners' key concern was 'the only object of any importance

A cleared coppice of ash and oak in the Wychwood area today.

to the public, the protection and maintenance of the timber'. Since the monarch no longer hunted deer, the only *raison d'être* for the existence of the Royal Forests was to provide a continuous supply of timber for the Royal Navy. However, although it was the most conveniently placed of all the Royal Forests, except Waltham in Essex, for transporting timber to the naval dockyards, not a single tree had been provided during the whole period from 1700 to 1786. According to the 1547 Act for the Preservation of Timber, and the terms of the lease of the royal coppices to the Duke, the coppices should contain twelve timber trees per acre; yet there was only an average of five. There were twice as many oaks in the open forest as in the coppices, which showed that the careless cutting of the underwood, when the coppices were cleared, caused even more damage than the deer. Thomas Morris, Keeper of Roger's Hill Walk, said that a previous wood-ward, Mr Chandler, who had died 26 years before, had deliberately cut young oaks in the coppices to increase the underwood – the underwood belonged to the lessee. Trees were also frequently cut in the coppices to provide browse for the deer. The deer would eat the twiggy wood from the branches and tops; what was left was one of the keepers' perquisites.

Things were even worse in the open forest, outside the coppices:

There is no appearance of young oaks, or tillers, coming up, under 20 years growth, in the open parts of the forest, nor ever will be, nor ever can be any, unless a stop is put to cutting the bushes in the forest, and the lopping and cutting the young trees, which is done in open day, and carried away often in waggons, in the night, avowedly and without regard; insomuch as almost all the covert for young wood growing up is destroyed; that the forest is overrun with swine; and it is feared that neither the swine, nor even the deer, are kept out of the King's coppices, where good timber is growing.

The Commissioners attributed the poor state of the Forest to the complicated and divided system of management that had developed over time – 'a perplexed mixture of rights'. The deer and the open forest were under the care of the Ranger (the Duke) in perpetuity; the underwood in the coppices was leased to the Duke by the Department for Crown Lands; while the timber in the coppices was the responsibility of the Surveyor-General of Woods. But neither government department had any representative in the Forest. The Woodward who cared for all the woodland, open or coppiced, was, like the Keepers, appointed by and answerable to the Duke as Ranger. The same Woodward was also responsible for the 12 coppices that the Duke owned in the Purlieu, and the Commission noted that these were better cared for than the King's coppices.

The Woodward in 1792, Solomon Goffe, had been in office for 26 years; since he was now 83 years old his son-in-law Robert Pratt carried out his duties. As Pratt told the Commission, the salary was only £30 a year, and the post carried with it no lodge, land or other perquisites. Among the most fascinating features of the 1792 Report are the statements taken from those who saw the Forest from ground level, the Keepers, the Woodward and the Billman. Two of them are unable to sign their names, and just put their mark, which tells something of their social status. For the first time we can hear the voice of ordinary Forest workers, learn something of their daily work and conditions, and hear some of their complaints. Each Keeper has a Lodge, and a piece of meadow land, the hay from which was intended for the deer; but according to William Eeles of Patch Hill Walk, his meadow doesn't even provide enough hay for his horse. Their salaries range from £10 to £15 a year, but they enjoy numerous perks, including the skin, offal and shoulders of all deer killed under warrant, and the timber from trees cut to feed the deer.

They must have been well aware that all was not as it should be in the Forest, and worried that they might be blamed for this. There is an understandable defensiveness about some of their comments, and they feel helpless before their social superiors. Thomas Morris, Keeper of Roger's

Hill Walk, and Joseph Pratley of Potter's Hill Walk, both refer to the problem of oxen. They know that these have never been allowed into the Forest, but some years before a Mr. Nutt of Minster Lovell had sent his oxen to pasture there, and they had not felt able to stop him. Others had since followed suit, 'to the great injury of the young trees and young deer, nor can the keepers prevent this from being continued, unless supported by the Government, or the Duke of Marlborough, in resisting it.' This support, they must have felt, was lacking.

Ranger's Lodge, like South Lawn Lodge a gentleman's residence, had been occupied for some 20 years by Admiral Pigott, with the Duke's permission. He too had upset the Forest officials. He had taken over a meadow from the Keeper of Shorthampton Walk, Thomas Gray, promising to 'allow him something handsome in lieu of it'. For some years Gray had been given eight guineas a year, but in recent years nothing. Nor, as we know, did the Admiral consult the Woodward about cutting timber for firewood, but got his servants to go and cut whatever was needed.

The picture uncovered by the Commissioners was one of decay and dereliction, and the reasons were clear to them:

> The rights of the Crown have not indeed been regularly exercised, nor to their full extent, and this is easily to be accounted for; none of our Kings, for a considerable length of time, have taken the Diversion of the Chase in the Forests situated at a distance from the Royal Residence; and from the number and extent of the forests, a small annual supply of deer from each was sufficient to answer the demand for the King's table...
>
> The consequence has been in this, as well as other forests, that those officers to whom only the custody of the deer has been committed have at length been led to consider them as their own, and to look upon the forbearance of the crown as a admission of their right.
>
> Little chance remains of any succession of timber in this forest, unless some change of management shall take place.

Their proposed solution was to buy out the Duke.

> Situated, as this Forest is, near to the Thames [and thus with good access to naval dockyards] ... we cannot avoid recommending that this part of the ancient demesnes of the Crown should be preserved

as a <u>nursery of timber</u>, & this can only be effected by an arrangement with the Duke of Marlborough, either for the purchase of his grant of the Rangership & lease of the Coppices, or for the continuation of the grant of the office of Ranger with right to all the game in the Forest <u>except the deer</u>, which, for the preservation & increase of timber, we are of the opinion <u>should be removed</u>. [with full compensation to the Duke] The lease of the coppices should not be renewed, and the land appropriated to the growth of timber.

They also proposed that the open Forest should be gradually enclosed, and timber allowed to grow there, that acorns should be planted in the coppices, and that the young trees should be effectively protected against pasturing cattle. A resident Woodward, answerable to the Crown, should be appointed to see that all this was done.

The Duke was not responsive, however, and in the following years only a few lesser recommendations were carried out. In 1797 John Robinson (Surveyor of Woods and Forests) recommended to the Treasury thinning out the old trees and others not fit for naval use, and selling them by auction. This would allow the younger trees to grow – 'there is a great quantity of young oak trees coming forward in succession.' Throughout the 1790s decayed and 'unimproving' trees, and some Navy oaks, were felled, and the planting of acorns began in 1795. At the turn of the century large numbers of trees were felled for sale – 570 ash and beech and 1200 oak in 1799, and 1004 oaks in 1800. As we move into the nineteenth century felling continued. In 1809 (the year of Arthur Young's visit) warrants were issued to fell 600 oaks for the Navy; in 1810, 490; in 1811, 500; in 1812, 510; and so it continued through into the 1820s, though with a reduction to 300 – 400 a year after the coming of peace in 1815. About half the trees came from the open forest, the rest were felled coppice by coppice, in 1809 Notteridge, in 1810 Kingswood, in 1811 Roustage, and so on.

In 1810 the administration of Crown lands was changed, and the Surveyor-General of Woods and Forests was replaced by three Commissioners for Woods, Forests and Land Revenue. The government began actively to promote a policy of disafforesting and enclosure. In 1817 the ancient post, long a sinecure, of Chief Justice in Eyre, was finally abolished. When Lord Churchill inherited Cornbury the same year he asked the Commission for Woods and Forests to repair the wall, or to bring pressure on the adjoining landowners to carry out this traditional responsibility. Unfortunately for him one of the Commissioners was the noted reformer William Huskisson, who responded by sending a team to inspect the Forest. They found that the wall at the Finstock end of the Forest had never been built, that the wall on Shipton Downs was very defective, and that the Forest gates were usually left open. In these circumstances, Huskisson wrote, there was no benefit in repairing the rest, and Lord Churchill's request was therefore refused. Moreover, he wrote, 'from the whole tenor of their [the inspectors] communication I am led to infer that the Forest is in a most unprofitable state...to your Lordship as Ranger, to the Crown as owner of the timber, compared to what it might be made if an enclosure or division could be brought about.'[2]

Lord Churchill now began to feel the pressure for reform. Various proposals were made for removing the deer, and enclosing the whole Forest. Under one offer, Lord Churchill would be granted one eighteenth part of the Forest in return for his rights as Ranger. Another more detailed proposal was that the open forest should be divided equally between the Crown (with 150 acres for Lord Churchill), and the Lords of adjoining manors and other free-holders. Of the coppices three quarters would go to the Crown (with a share for the Ranger) and the rest to Lords of the Manors etc. These proposals must have seemed insultingly inadequate compensation to Lord Churchill for his immemorial rights, and 'after much correspondence and verbal discussion the scheme was strongly objected to by the Ranger.'

In 1831, however, the 70-year lease of the royal coppices, made to the Duke of Marlborough in 1762, terminated. As the Commission had threatened in 1817, it was not renewed. The management of the coppices reverted to the Crown, who installed their own Woodward to look after them, and the Crown's other interests in Wychwood. Now, for the first time, the Commission had its own man on the ground, and as the Great Reform Bill was making its tortuous way through Parliament, in Wychwood things moved towards a final confrontation between the reformers of the Commission, and a Lord Churchill entrenched in the defence of his inherited rights.

Battle was joined in 1833 over the timber in the open forest, which was claimed by both parties. The Crown Woodward, now resident, complained that Lord Churchill had cut timber there; and when more was felled by order of the Crown, Lord Churchill's solicitor served notice on the Crown

Deer in Cornbury Park.

Agent not to remove or sell it. Lord Churchill was prepared to put the matter to arbitration, but his notion of compensation (£100,000) differed so much from that of the Crown (£10,000), that the Attorney-General 'refused decidedly' to contemplate it. G.A.Crawley, solicitor to the Commission, was instructed to proceed against Lord Churchill in 1834, which he did by challenging every right that Lord Churchill claimed in the Forest, not merely his claim to the timber. There followed a lawsuit of Dickensian length and complexity, which lasted for the rest of Lord Churchill's life, as he doubtless intended. Meanwhile all tree felling was suspended, which deprived both parties of any income from the sale of timber, and also led to further deterioration in the state of the Forest.

Mr Crawley told a later enquiry that at every stage of the suit he had had to use 'compulsory measures' to get Lord Churchill to respond, and Lord Churchill was indeed defiant in his resistance to the spirit of the age. The Commission's interest was in the timber, and the main enemy to the timber was the deer. He responded to a query from the Crown in 1834:

> with respect to the number of deer killed for my own use, it is impos-
> sible for me to make any return of them, as the entire use & control
> of the deer of this forest, deducting those killed under the warrants,
> has always been enjoyed as a right by me & my predecessors ... a
> right which has been exercised for centuries without interruption &
> which has never been disputed until this year.

He then claims credit for increasing their number:

The stock of deer now existing here was raised to its present state by my exertions & at my cost, for at the time when I entered upon the office of ranger the number of deer in the Forest was extremely small and ... insufficient for the proper service of the Crown & other warrants.

Certainly, the numbers had increased. From about 1,000 at the time of the 1792 Report, by 1843 there were 1,570, and five years later 1,900. Finally, he reintroduced red deer to Wychwood for the first time since the mid-eighteenth century, bringing about forty head from Lord Redesdale's estate at Batsford Park in Gloucestershire. This was a flamboyant challenge to the Commission – not only could red deer jump over any coppice fence, but they are voracious eaters, consuming their own body weight in fodder every ten to fourteen days.

Among the Watney papers in the Oxfordshire Record Office is the 'Wychwood Forest Venison Book' for 1833-42, in which are recorded all the deer officially killed, by whom, on whose warrant, and who received the carcass. In 1833 the total was 45 Bucks, 72 Does, and 86 Fawns, the latter merely being marked 'sold or given away'. Some were killed by Crown Warrant – these went to the Royal Larder, various State Offices, and individuals including Lord Palmerston. Then there were the Composition Warrants, providing deer for landowners in the Purlieu, mainly the Bishop of Winchester and Lord Redesdale. The bulk of the deer, however, were killed by Ranger's Warrant, and their destinations are very varied. A few went to the Dukes of Beaufort and Marlborough, some to the Deputy Ranger (C.Henderson) and the Verderers (Colonel Parker and Mr J.H.Langston). Others were sent to various local groups – the Bailiffs of Witney, the Magistrates' Clerks, the Oxford Race Dinner, the Witney Blanket Company, the Ascot Prosecution Club – and one, oddly, to 'the Regulator's coachman'. Lesser folk only got part of a carcass: one buck was shared between Mr. Albright of Charlbury, Mr. Gomm of Ascot, Mr. Maycock of Ranger's Lodge, and Charles Pratley of Swinbrook.

After 1834 there are no entries until 1842, when they are incomplete and scrappy. The warrants are not always specified; and the fawns are now divided up between the keepers and neighbouring farmers. It suggests that control over the Forest was declining, and that no one cared very much what went on there as legal arguments dragged on. It would certainly be hard to argue that the maintenance of the deer herd was a vital national interest.

In 1836 Lord Churchill filed a counter-plea, and the next two years were taken up in collecting 'voluminous documentation'. Much of this was done, at the Commission's request, by Stacey Grimaldi, a London lawyer and antiquary, and descendant of the Doges of Genoa, who researched the history of the Forest back to the time of Domesday. Grimaldi's *Report upon the Rights of the Crown in the Forest of Wychwood in the County of Oxford* was presented in 1838, and opens with the blunt statement that 'with very few and trifling exceptions his Lordship's claims are unfounded.' In April 1840 proceedings began against Lord Churchill, who applied for a postponement until the following February. He then withdrew all his previous arguments, which derived from his rights as Ranger, and put forward a new case, based upon his manorial rights in Langley, Leafield and Ramsden. (Grimaldi had already asserted that these three manors did not exist, and that their lands were all part of the Manor of Shipton.) The Crown responded in 1842, Lord Churchill replied the following year, and 'consultations' were still continuing when Lord Churchill died in 1845. The cost of the lawsuit to the government, between the years 1833 and 1847, amounted to £7,586.

The second Lord Churchill, however, was more amenable than his father, and maybe more open to the economic arguments for enclosure. Soon after succeeding he withdrew many of the family's claims, and expressed the wish to 'enter into amicable negotiation' for the settlement of the rest. Soon he allowed the Crown to cut the browsewood in the coppices, a claim his father had vigorously resisted. The way towards disafforesting was now open, though it would be another ten years before the process would be complete. A further parliamentary enquiry was held in 1848, to gather evidence on what could best be done with the Forest.

The Report of this Enquiry shows that opinion had shifted away from encouraging the preservation of the timber, which had been the main concern of the previous generation. The 1792 Report had envisaged Wychwood becoming a 'nursery of timber', a great oak forest stretching from Cornbury to Burford. When the Commission of Woods and Forests had taken over the coppices in 1831 they had planted young oak saplings from a local nursery, each time a coppice was cleared. But now Abram Rawlinson, Lord Churchill's agent, said that the prices of timber, underwood and bark were all declining, and once the railway was built the underwood would scarcely be worth the cutting. The railway would bring coal to replace firewood; and Brunel was already building his iron ships, which suggested that there was little future for 'Navy timber'.

Ironically, the timber, especially the oak, was now in excellent condition, though opinions as to its value varied. Rawlinson estimated its value as '£10,000 easily', but the Deputy Surveyor of Windsor Forest, Charles Maslin, who had been cutting timber in Wychwood since 1814, thought it might be worth £50-70,000. However, William Downes, agent to Earl de Grey and a number of other landowners, gave a figure of £150,000 for the timber, and £280-300,000 for the Forest as a whole. These varied estimates of its value are startling, though Maslin makes it clear that he is referring only to timber in the open forest, not the coppices.

The public interest no longer required nurseries of timber, and minds were turning instead towards clearing the woodland altogether and using the land for agriculture. Most of the Forest was fit for cultivation, said Rawlinson; the value of the timber would more than cover the costs of clearance, and if cleared it would provide more secure employment for local people. Rawlinson was Clerk to the Chipping Norton Poor Law Union, and agreed that the Wychwood parishes were the poorest in the area, since local people could only get seasonal work in the Forest, when the coppices were cut.

William Downes had a less drastic solution. He would remove the deer, which were 'perfectly destructive to the property', and clear the under-growth and rubbish; but where the trees were 'healthy and handsome' he would 'parkify' it – lay it down to grass which would not injure the beauty of the country, and at the same time enclose and retain much of the timber. The undergrowth could be cleared, grass grown under the trees and let out for pasture. He reckoned that every hundred acres of enclosed forest would provide permanent employment for four labourers, in addition to other trades such as carpenters.

The economic arguments for action were strong. The average net income produced by the Forest in the first half of the century was only 2/2d per acre, and this was declining since no timber had been cut at all during the lawsuit. Its value as farmland, however, would be 25/- to 26/- an acre. In the end, given the declining value of timber, Downes' compromise solu-tion did not find favour, and the centuries-old conflict between the needs of the deer and the trees was resolved by doing away with both. In July 1853, an Act for the Disafforesting of Whichwood was passed. The offices of Ranger, Launder, Four Bailiffs, etc., were abolished, the deer were to be

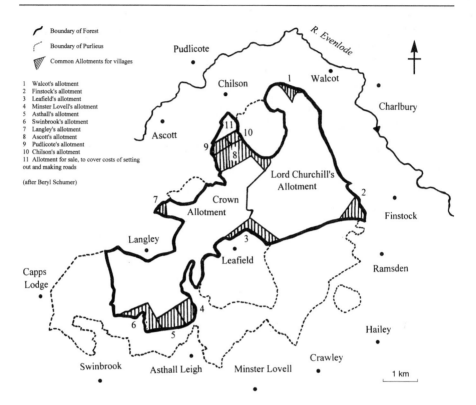

Map showing the distribution of land at disafforesting.

removed or destroyed within two years, and the timber on the common land cut down. New roads were to be laid out, and all other roads and ways through the Forest closed. There would be a new parish of Whichwood, and a maximum of 10 acres was to be set aside for building a church, school and parsonage.

Three commissioners were appointed to divide up and allocate the land between those who had claims to it. Lord Churchill was awarded Ranger's Lodge, together with about 1500 acres of forest land next to Cornbury Park. These have been part of the Cornbury Estate ever since. The ordinary commoners, descendants of those who had pastured their cattle in the Forest for centuries, were granted pieces of land in compensation; but these were often too small, and the land too poor, to be of any value, and many were soon sold and amalgamated into larger holdings. John Kibble recorded, 'I have heard my father say very plain things about the injustice done to these people, but there was no hope for it, "take your worthless bit of land or nothing", seems to have been the rule.' The church, school, and parsonage were never built; in 1860 Whichwood became part of Leafield for ecclesiastical purposes, though it remained a civil parish.

The first act of the Commissioners was to have 10 miles of roads built, 30 feet wide with a 15-foot stone track. All were bordered by stone walls. This was financed by the sale of an area of the Forest at Smallstones. Then the clearing of the Crown allotment of 2937 acres began. First the deer were killed; not only the keepers, but sportsmen from the whole neighbourhood were brought in to complete the slaughter. 'Many a sportsman, whose largest game had hitherto been blackbirds, could afterwards boast of the number of deer that had fallen to his fowling-piece.'

These are the words of C. Belcher, who became tenant of the newly created Potter's Hill Farm, and whose account of the clearance is the most detailed, and also reflects most vividly the mood of utilitarian triumphalism with which it was carried out. The Forest, in his view, was no more than waste – 'unreclaimed forest land, dense, dark and gloomy; its silence seldom disturbed, except by the axe of the woodman, the gun of the game-keeper, or the stealthy tread of the deer-stealer.' When the deer had been killed, many hundreds of men and boys were employed to clear the land,

> some cutting the light wood and laying it in drift, some tying the fire-wood into faggots, some preparing the larger pieces for posts and fencing, and others busy felling the timber trees or stripping off the bark. Gradual and steady was the advance, like that of an invading army; such an army, however, as might have been looked on with pleasure, even by a member of the Peace Society.

Fowler's Tree-throwing Machine was used to deal with many of the smaller trees and bushes, using a windlass, cables and chains to drag dozens at a time to the ground. Then the stumps had to be grubbed up – no easy task, given the thick networks of roots, not only of the trees that had just been felled, but also of those felled many years before; but 'stout tools, and the strong arms of Englishmen, are seldom overcome by difficulties.'

The profit on the timber, once the costs of clearance had been deducted, was £16,531; the further costs of grubbing up the tree-stumps, putting up farmhouses and associated buildings, fencing, drainage etc, came to £26,983, so that there was a net outlay by the Crown of £10,452. But the annual rental income from the seven farms on the cleared land would amount to £5,104, compared with the average annual income from the Forest of £1,813. This, wrote Belcher, 'must be highly satisfactory to us as patriotic Englishmen and loyal subjects.' He continues with sentiments that would have been applauded by Arthur Young:

> Formerly, when deer and game abounded in the coverts, deer-stealers and poachers, idlers and thieves, were numerous around...fortunately the chief incentive to such vicious courses died out with the last deer; honest employment can now be obtained on the new farms; each season brings its appointed work, and none need be idle who wish to be busy. Poets and painters may sigh because some fine woodland scenery has been swept away; but, of what consequence is a magnificent view, when compared with that plenty which has taken the place of poverty, or those habits of industry now firmly established, where dissipation and crime once abounded?

The clearance had been carried out with impressive speed: it began in October 1856, and was completed by January 1858, the first crops, of oats, swedes and turnips, being sown later that year. Yet even when cleared, the land was far from easy to work. Many tree stumps had not been grubbed up, there were large areas of fern and bramble, ancient pits where stone had been quarried long ago, reappeared to view; and the banks and ditches that had surrounded the old coppices had to be levelled. Belcher used burning and the breast-plough to clear his own land, and appears to have had greater success than his neighbours, but it took even him several years to level the six miles of old coppice bank.

Official opinion of the time admired 'the marvellous rapidity of the execution' of this 'truly national' work, but a strong sense of loss was felt in the immediate locality. John Kibble witnesses to its effect on the villagers:

> When the Forest was enclosed it was a sad blow to many who lived on its borders, for some of them got a great part of their living out of the Forest. Burdens of wood for firing, fallen branches, and furze were brought and sold to those who could buy. In spring wild birds' eggs helped to make many a nice pudding... In the season nuts were gathered and sold for the extraction of nut oil, others were saved for sale.

A 1990 study of Leafield workers by Keith Chandler shows the disruptive effect on the community most closely connected with the Forest. In the

1851 census 53% of Leafield men had occupations associated with the Forest. By 1871 this had been reduced to 4%, while the proportion of agricultural labourers had risen from 22% to 62%. The years between saw a more than average migration out of the village, as woodmen moved away to places where they could still exercise their traditional skills. However, once the immediate crisis had passed, agriculture offered more permanent and stable employment than the Forest had. Over the twenty years between 1851 and 1871 the population of Leafield rose by some 7% and this is perhaps a sign that the change had made it a more prosperous place.

These shifts in population and employment also helped to destroy the traditional culture. Chandler based his study on those families whose members were Morris Men; but as the dancers moved away, and their annual journeys to London ceased, the dancing for which Leafield was famous came to an end. The last set was danced there in the early 1860s, and by 1870 it had ceased throughout the whole area.

Enclosure also had an impact on foxhunting, and the Heythrop huntsman, Jem Hills, described how the foxes were confused by the destruction of their familiar coverts:

> It's all grubbed up and the deer killed, red and fallow; we used to go through hundreds of them on the drives. Lords Churchill and Redesdale have left only a bit of it at the top and the bottom, where the foxes must fly. The old foresters [foxes] get puzzled, and they can't dwell; they get lost and dare not touch certain covers and go downwind. It's a blackthorn hazel cover, with grass. They used to put a six-foot hedge, with thorns outside, to keep the deer out. The foxes smeused, and the hounds would jump at the fences and lose their eyes or get staked and drop into the ditch; that's done away with now, that's one little comfort, but there's no badger hunting.

The more leisured classes had lost their familiar picnic sites, and it must have been one of them – or maybe one of the 'poets or painters' so despised by Farmer Belcher – who wrote to *The Times* in 1859 as 'The Ghost of Whichwood', provoked by the self-congratulatory tone of an editorial praising the clearance. 'My character was never called in question,' he or she claimed. The only people 'who wandered through my domain were a few harmless gipsies, against whom no one complained. The farmer was well pleased and satisfied with his rights of common.' Yet now the Forest

'Turnips and stone walls': the landscape after the disafforesting, near Kingstanding Farm.

had been replaced by 'turnips and stone walls', as 'My Lords Churchill and Redesdale, whom I had long fostered, deserted me in my long hour of need, and gain and greed carried the day.'

Certainly poets and painters, and any lover of natural scenery, had much to regret. The large, bare, rectangular fields remain a bleak substitute for the ancient woodland. Nor, in the longer term, was the effect of the clearing nearly as positive as Belcher and others believed. The diaries of John Simpson Calvertt, who farmed Langley and Fairspear farms in the later nineteenth century, were published under the title of 'Rain and Ruin', which tells its own story. The problem was not just the weather, or the prolonged agricultural slump, but that the farmland itself was of such variable, and mostly poor quality. Later, in 1916, John Orr reported one farmer on the old Forest land saying that in a fifty-acre field he found six different kinds of soil, which made cultivation difficult. 'He thinks it was a mistake that the trees were ever grubbed, since the return on the capital expenditure has been inadequate.' On the other hand the surviving area of Forest, in the Cornbury Estate, still showed how well suited the land was for trees. In the 1950s this was subjected to closer scientific examination and, more than a century later, evidence of its mistreatment during the eighteenth and early nineteenth centuries was still apparent. The agronomist W.H. Pearsall toured the estate, and found evidence of severe overgrazing, especially on the valley sides and outer edges. Another survey found that Dog's Mercury (*Mercurialis perennis*) dominates the Forest floor to an extent virtually unknown elsewhere. This plant is poisonous to animals, and overgrazing over a long period had destroyed all competing species.

Another victim of enclosure was the Whitsun Hunt, whose origins may go back to Saxon times. The people of Burford and Witney, and a few neighbouring villages, had the right to hunt deer in the Forest on Whit Sunday, and the ceremonies associated with this custom show its ancient origin. A Whitsun Lord and Lady were chosen, and the townsfolk summoned by horns made from peeled bark. In 1593 the Privy Council banned the hunt at the Burford end of the Forest, because of the plague. 'Many people,' they wrote to the Burford Bailiffs, 'of divers Townes whereof some are infected will be drawn together to Ye hassard of many of her Mat^{yes} subjects. These are therefor in her Mat^{yes} name to require Yw to forbear your hunting there for this year...' In recompense, the people of Burford would be sent two bucks from the forest. Although the ban was said to be for one year only, it continued in force indefinitely; and the gift of two bucks was made each year until the disafforesting, when it was commuted for a payment of £150.

In fact, it seems that the Burford hunt was not suppressed so easily. When Charles I revived the Forest Court in the 1630s Richard Somerby 'called Whitsun Lord of Burford' was called before it, since he 'and other inhabitants of Burford with their dogs chased and killed four deer of the said Lord the King and carried them away.' But eventually it was replaced by a new custom, and the churchwardens and people of Burford processed on Whit Sunday to Capp's Lodge for a picnic, and elected a boy and girl as King and Queen of the feast. But this was put down in its turn in 1827 by a newly-arrived evangelical curate 'in consequence of the gross improprieties it led to on such a solemn feast of the church as Whit Sunday.'

At the western end of the Forest, though, the Witney hunt continued until the middle of the nineteenth century, and the first Lord Churchill himself occasionally took part with his staghounds. But by now the hunting (one buck each for Witney, Hailey and Crawley) was secondary to the dancing, drinking and fighting that marked these occasions; and for festivity there was major competition from the Forest Fair held in September on Newell Plain. Though so vividly remembered, this was of comparatively recent origin. It had started in the 1790s when some Witney Methodists, in disgust at the goings-on during the Witney Wakes

The Grand Vista.

Week, escaped with their friends for a picnic in the peace of the Forest. Unfortunately for them, it was not long before others took up the idea, and soon everything they had tried to avoid followed them there. By the 1820s the Forest Fair attracted up to twenty thousand merrymakers, and the Plain was filled with refreshment booths, clothing and sweet stalls, exhibitions of pig-faced ladies and two-headed calves, Wombwell's menagerie, and the Vauxhall Dancing Saloon, illuminated in the evening by 500 coloured lamps. The Yeomanry Band played, and in the afternoon the gentry paraded in their carriages – the Duke and Duchess of Marlborough, Lord and Lady Churchill, attended by coachmen and footmen in scarlet coats, red plush breeches, white stockings and cockades.

But there was a darker side to the Fair. Like the Whitsun Hunt, it had become the recognised occasion for grudge fights between local men. 'Did a ploughman have a quarrel with one of his fellow labourers? Nothing more was said at the time other than, I'll see thee at Forest Fair. See each other they did, and under the great trees in Wychwood they fought it out.' The Forest was extra-parochial and so not subject to parish constables; the Oxfordshire Constabulary would not be founded until 1859. There was some harsh vigilantism:

Rough and ready was the law enforced on the Plain. I saw a pickpocket who had been detected, hustled down the bank and ducked three times till nearly dead, he lay on the bank the very personification of abject despair.

The Cornbury gamekeepers were sworn in as special constables, and Lord Churchill, as magistrate, would be busy the next day, but there was not much they could do as the crowds grew to tens of thousands.

Lord Churchill had tried to ban the Fair in 1831, without effect; but what finally made the Fair intolerable to him and others was the coming of the railway in 1853. First came the navvies building the line, who brought terror into the whole neighbourhood, and particularly so at Fair time. Then, once the line was opened, it brought visitors more numerous than ever, many from outside the neighbourhood and even harder for the temporary constables to control. The last time the Fair was held, in 1855, more than a dozen special excursion trains arrived at Charlbury station, and their occupants poured through the town, into Cornbury Park, past the House, and along the Grand Vista, to Newell Plain, to return much later in various states of inebriation. It is not surprising that respectable citizens locked their children up at home until the Fair should be over. In 1856, however, Lord Churchill became the owner of Newell Plain, and promptly banned the Fair. There was some difficulty to start with in getting the ban observed, but finally he had deep trenches dug across the approach roads, and prevented any of the wagons or caravans approaching the plain.

But one far more ancient Forest tradition continues to the present day. It presumably has its origin in pilgrimages to holy wells, such as Ladywell in Wilcote. There is no record of it from earlier centuries, but at the beginning of the twentieth century the people of the ancient Forest settlement of Fieldtown (Leafield) would still make their way into the Forest on Palm Sunday. They brought with them bottles of strong medicinal liquid, made of liquorice and peppermint, to dilute with spring water. The correct well to visit was the 'Wussell', or Worts Well, whose name evokes traditions of healing herbs; but many would go on to the Iron Well, the chalybeate spring near the Wilderness. Palm Sunday remains the one day of the year when that section of the ancient Forest is open, though few if any bring medicinal liquid with them.

Notes
1 Oxfordshire County Archive, Apl/III/iii/7
2 Oxfordshire County Archive, Misc. Watney VIII/i/1

8

The Cornbury Estate

If the first Lord Churchill, galloping with his scarlet-and-yellow uniformed Yeomanry through Wychwood, joining in the Whitsun Hunt with his staghounds, and resisting reform tooth and nail, typifies the Regency era (he even died in Brighton), his son, Francis George Spencer, second Lord Churchill, is far more characteristic of the Victorian age. Born in 1802, he was a diplomat in his youth, serving as an attaché in Lisbon and Vienna. But he soon returned to Cornbury where, according to his grandson, 'he settled down early to the life of a scholar. Greek and Latin classics were his subjects, and he carried on an enormous correspondence with classical scholars, but as far as I know he never contributed anything to the scholarly literature of the day.' He was loyal enough to the military tradition of the family, however, to be Lieutenant-Colonel of the Yeomanry Cavalry at the time of his father's death, and in 1857 he took over its command.

In 1849 he married Lady Jane Conyngham, daughter of the Marquess Conyngham. She was half his age, a lively, sharp-tongued woman, who became Lady of the Bedchamber to Queen Victoria in 1855. She held this post for the rest of her life, becoming one of the Queen's closest and most trusted friends. She spent summers at Balmoral, and was the Queen's companion on incognito jaunts through the glens. Later she went with her to Germany and Italy; and was at her side in 1872 when a young Fenian pointed a pistol at the Queen, who threw herself in terror into Lady Churchill's arms. Queen Victoria became godmother to the Churchills' son and grandson, both of whom were christened Victor in her honour.

Having negotiated the disafforesting, Lord Churchill incorporated his allotment of Wychwood into the Cornbury Estate, and by 1862 it was all enclosed. But this part of the Forest was not cleared, as the Crown allotment had been, and it is thanks to Lord Churchill and his successors that it remains today. Not only Wychwood was cleared in the mid-century, but much other woodland in the area – the Purlieu coppices in Crawley and Hailey, Minster Wood, and Lee's Rest Wood in Charlbury, for example – and Lord Churchill could have followed suit and turned the land over to cultivation. It might well have seemed in his interest to do so since by the time of his death in 1886 the estate was heavily mortgaged, and being entailed for three generations, none of it could be sold off.

As well as being more amenable to reform, he had a typically Victorian paternalistic social conscience. Shortly after inheriting he cleared two of his own coppices, Studley, near Leafield, and Boynal, above Shipton, and turned them into 'Fields of Industry' – allotments to be let to villagers at a reduced rent. However, the main object of the Churchills' charitable concern was Finstock. They owned most of the land there and held the great tithes, and since it is close to the main working area of the estate – the quarry, the sawmill, and the kitchen garden – it was presumably the home of some estate workers and a natural focus for others. The first Lord Churchill had given land for a church at Finstock in 1841: the first entry in its marriage register is that of his daughter Elizabeth Spencer, and all the family were buried there. In 1866 his son presented the church with a pulpit, lectern and choir stalls in memory of the first Lady Churchill. Lord Churchill supported a free school in the 1840s, and in 1860 gave land for a National (Church of England) School. Lady Churchill took a strong personal interest in the school, and went visiting among the villagers. John Kibble, whose father was a Finstock stonemason, wrote that she 'was always kind to my grandmother, used to call and chat with her...I never saw Lady Churchill but she was wearing earrings made like little black tea kettles'.

Lord Churchill's concern for Finstock people extended to their welfare organisations, and he was the manager of the Finstock branch of the Oxfordshire Friendly Society, which became known locally as 'Lord Churchill's Club'. According to Jesse Clifford he was responsible for getting an Act passed, preventing old style benefit clubs, often based at local inns, from spending their funds on bands and feasting – this brought a swift end to the Charlbury clubs based at the Bell and the Crown. Lord Churchill's club did have its annual dinner, in the school, but its funds were well protected, and when it finally dissolved, having only three or four members, there was a tidy sum left for each of them.

The 2nd Lord Churchill and Lady Churchill.

Lady Churchill's connections brought occasional royal visitors to Cornbury. Princess Alexandra of Wales came in 1871, to be greeted as she passed through Charlbury by flags and pealing church bells; she came again in 1881 with Prince Leopold. Queen Victoria herself paid a visit in December 1886, after the death of Lord Churchill, to condole with her close friend. This time there were no peals of bells as the Queen made her way to Cornbury from the Royal Train at Charlbury station, and the local people lined the streets in silent sympathy.

The third Lord Churchill, Victor Albert Francis Charles Spencer, inherited his estate when he was only 22. It was heavily encumbered with debt; there were rumours the following summer that the mortgagers were about to foreclose, and in August it was let to Llewellyn Wynne, of Steeple Aston. For an annual rent of £1,100 Wynne occupied the House, Park, and Ranger's Lodge, enjoyed rights of grazing and shooting in Wychwood, and shooting rights over the rest of the estate. One clause in the lease stipulated that on its expiry there should be at least 70 head of fallow deer in the Park, 'unless prevented by the herd being attacked by rabies.' By 1890 Wynne happily reported that he had increased the number of deer from 120 to 200:

'They are very fine animals, extra large in fact, and they run very wild, especially the does.' He was also required 'to leave a fair head of game in the Forest and coverts, and keep down hares and rabbits.'[1]

Lord Churchill, who had married very soon after his Father's death, lived in London, where he was serving with the Coldstream Guards. Though Cornbury was let, Wychwood was still his to manage, and he set about felling and replanting sizeable areas of the old Forest. 'Great alterations are taking place on Lord C.'s estate,' the local farmer John Simpson Calvertt wrote in his diary, 'part sold – much planted – and altogether much altered and improved.' All the oaks and 'smooth' wood near Cockshoot Hill were cut down, to be replaced with larch. More timber was cut near Cockshoot and Witley Hills in 1889, and the following year Calvertt recorded that 200,000 trees had been planted along the Leafield-Charlbury road and at the north end of Cockshoot Hill. There was also planting within the Park, of oaks, sycamores, spruce, and scotch firs.

Wynne was a man with political ambitions, – he stood three times, but without success, as Conservative candidate for North Oxfordshire – and was keen to make himself known and liked. During his time at Cornbury the Park was open to the public as never before, and witnessed all kinds of unprecedented activities. The Banbury Rovers Football Club came to play, to be followed by the Banbury Old Quoit Club. When the Cornbury Lakes froze over, anyone who wished was welcome to skate – an invitation repeated every year in that age of hard winters – and sometimes there were torchlight processions on the ice. The coming years would see the Park hosting Bank Holiday Galas, Monster Conservative Demonstrations, and Primrose League Fetes, and even the Charlbury Total Abstinence Society held its annual picnic there. From 1891 the Whit Monday Sports were held on the lawn in front of the House, stalls, roundabouts and shooting galleries were set up, and the day rounded off with dancing. The old Riding School was brought into use for performances by the Finstock Brass Band, and magic lantern shows. But Wynne provided more than just entertainment. He opened a soup kitchen during the winter, with food for about 30 poor families – 'the gratitude of the labouring classes towards the donor is very great,' noted the *Oxford Times* – and supported the allotment movement, inviting 40 allotment tenants to dine with him in 1888, and later providing land for 110 new allotments in Charlbury and Finstock. He also built an Orchid House in the Park, following a popular current fashion.

But all this came at a price, and both he and his landlord, Lord Churchill, were getting into deeper waters financially. In 1892 Lord Churchill bought Rolleston Hall in Leicestershire, a smaller estate than Cornbury, and moved towards selling the latter. (The entail on the estate had expired with his father's death.) The decision to sell the family estate disturbed him deeply, and in later years he would talk very emotionally about his old home. 'He had done a thorough job,' wrote his son, 'of selling house, forest, farms, library, family portraits, plate, everything which had piled up through a couple of centuries. Something that seemed curious and not explained…was the speed and violence with which he had gone at the dismantling of Cornbury.' There was a six-day sale in 1894, including 'the contents of 35 bedrooms, 120 oil paintings, and a large number of John Leech's pictures'. Even family heirlooms connected with the first Duke of Marlborough were auctioned, some ending up in German museums. This did not please the cousins at Blenheim.

In March 1895 Wynne went spectacularly bankrupt, having lost nearly £60,000 in Stock Market speculation, and accumulated total debts of over a quarter of a million pounds. His lease had already been terminated, but he had been offered further annual tenancies, which suggests that Lord Churchill had not finally made up his mind whether to sell. The future of Cornbury was now even more uncertain, and there were rumours that it would be let to a South African magnate, but in July 1896 the whole estate was offered for sale at auction. It was advertised as 'consisting of 3912 acres, comprising the House and Park, 1400 acres of woodland, Walcot, Shorthampton, Leafield, Smallstones, Finstock, Waterman's Lodge and Park Farms.' But it failed to reach its reserve price of £140,000 and the following month it was privately sold for £115,000 to the Chairman of the Dunlop Pneumatic Tyre Company, Harvey du Cros.

Du Cros' arrival marks a significant change in the history of Cornbury. Hitherto it had belonged to families whose wealth originated in political or military achievement – Danby, the Hydes, the Churchills – but its subsequent owners have been men whose money came from trade – tyres, brewing, and shipping. Cornbury thus reflects, if belatedly, the shift in power in the country at large during the nineteenth century, from the old landed gentry to the mercantile bourgeoisie. Du Cros had founded the Dunlop Company in 1889, together with the inventor of the pneumatic tyre

John Dunlop, and had just sold it for three million pounds to a financier, Ernest Terah Hooley, who as we shall see also helped him purchase Cornbury.

Known as the 'Napoleon of the Bicycle', du Cros was a self-consciously modern man, proud of being at the forefront of the transport revolution – he later described himself in *Who's Who* as 'an ardent motorist'. 'While others doubted the success of the pneumatic principle as applied to cycle tyres,' enthused *The Daily Mail*,

> including even the inventor, Mr Dunlop himself, Mr du Cros never wavered in his strong faith in the tyre which has made cycling and the cycle industry what it now is. The other day the employés of the Pneumatic Tyre Company presented Mr du Cros with a splendid service of plate and an illuminated address, as a token of the high appreciation in which he is held by them, and it is one of his most remarkable characteristics that he is able to inspire in those under him the warmest affection and the most self-sacrificing enthusiasm.

The effect of this was rather spoiled when his workers in Coventry came out on strike the next week. Since the company was making such huge profits they felt they should have a share, but du Cros disagreed. The strike leaders were sacked on the spot, and the rest were told that they were men of the labouring class and should be satisfied with 22s per week.

In its day Cornbury had witnessed impeachment and bankruptcy, but with the arrival of du Cros there is a whiff of sleaze. In March there was an enquiry into his selling company shares though another person; and at the end of the year the truth about the purchase of Cornbury became known, and led to Lord Churchill being the defendant in a suit brought against him by the agent for the sale. Du Cros, it seems, had bought the estate through Hooley, with whom the agent had had no contact, and who had paid Lord Churchill an extra £35,000. So Lord Churchill had received £150,000 for the estate, but had only paid the agent's commission on the £115,000 he had received from du Cros. Hooley boasted in the witness-box that he had dealings with du Cros worth ten million pounds, and that he had been negotiating for the purchase of fourteen large estates during the previous year. Lord Churchill won his case, but did not escape without some severe comments from the Bench. Lord Churchill 'had made statements which the facts did not fairly warrant, and the defendant's affidavit as to the price which he obtained for the property was, to say the least of it, misleading.

Cornbury House with du Cros' additions.

Such an affidavit ought not to have been drafted, and Lord Churchill ought never to have signed it.'

Du Cros was proud of being up-to-date, but on settling at Cornbury he also threw himself enthusiastically into the ancient role of Lord of the Manor. He revived the Manorial Court Leet in Charlbury, which had lapsed in 1888, and paid for a 'sumptuous repast' afterwards. Within a month of his arrival he took the chair at the opening of the town's new waterworks, and later paid for the fountain on the Playing Close, designed and built by John Kibble, which so economically commemorates the opening of the waterworks, and the Diamond Jubilee, and Queen Victoria's brief visit in 1886. In June over a thousand Dunlop employees, from London, Coventry and Birmingham, came to Cornbury on a works outing, and were welcomed at the station by the Charlbury Brass Band.

Both House and Park had been neglected during the previous few decades, and du Cros energetically set about their improvement. Newell Stream was cleaned down to the gravel base, Newell Pond was enlarged, retaining walls built and two new ponds created. In January 1897 Calvertt found 55 men cleaning out the ponds, and four sets of contractors – two or three hundred men in all – working on the House. A Surveyor's Report

'Four sets of contractors' working at Cornbury in 1897.

of 1898[2] notes that a new staircase was put in

> of a very handsome character. All the principal rooms were panelled,
> enriched ceilings put in, and new fireplaces and fittings of a very
> substantial character – the bedrooms have been rearranged and
> added to – hot and cold water supplied to most of the rooms and
> arrangements made for the ventilation of the house by hot and cold
> air. New lavatories and bathrooms have been fitted and a billiard
> room added.

The roof was releaded, new chimney stacks put in, an Engine House added
next to the Stable Yard with boilers and dynamos to provide electric light:
the house was wired for about 400 lights. In the Kitchen Gardens there
were built 'large ranges of Orchid Houses, Plant Houses, Vineries, Peach
Houses, Melon Houses with all the necessary accessories.' Most notably,
a single story portico, or *porte-cochère*, was added in the middle of the
Clarendon Wing, to provide the grand entrance that the House had always
lacked; and an Italianate Tower, modelled on that of Queen Victoria's
Osborne House, was erected in the inner angle of the Danby and

Clarendon wings. Dominating the view of the House, it was topped by an 'electric Ball-light', proclaiming that the modern world had reached Oxfordshire.

The cost of all this came to £53,963 'exclusive of £14,000 in wages'. Du Cros also built a new house at Southill for the estate manager, converted Ranger's Lodge for residential use, planted 50 acres of new woodland, and laid miles of wiring for protection against rabbits. Finally, he showed his firm intention of remaining at Cornbury by extending Finstock Churchyard to build a family mausoleum, which continued in use until the 1940s.

The Whit Monday Sports were still held in the Park, and in 1898 they attracted a large crowd, eager to see the new wonders of Cornbury. But the following week saw another bankruptcy, that of du Cros' business associate, Terah Hooley. No sooner had du Cros completed Cornbury's transformation than he had to put it back on the market. He moved to a more modest estate near Wallingford, but kept up some connection with the area, as late as 1905 inviting local tradesmen to spend a day at his new home.

In 1901 the Cornbury Estate was bought by Vernon James Watney, of the Watney brewing family, and as with du Cros, it was the profit from a recent business deal that provided the funds. His grandfather, James Watney (1800-1884) had established the family name, building up a large brewery business in London in the first half of the nineteenth century. His son, also James, and a Tory M.P., had converted the family firm into a limited company on his father's death, but died himself two years later, leaving the 26-year-old Vernon, and his younger brother Claude, to carry on the business. By the 1890s Vernon was chairman of a burgeoning enterprise which was actively buying up other breweries throughout London and beyond. In 1898 two other family-owned London breweries, Combe's and Reid's, were planning a merger, which would have made them the largest brewery in the capital; Watney suggested that he should join with them, and the even larger firm of Watney, Combe, Reid and Co. was created, to become one of the most important brewery companies in the country.

The new company was headed by Combe's Chairman, Sir Cosmo Bonsor, who would run it for thirty years. Vernon Watney took the opportunity offered by the merger to retire from full-time business, though he remained on the Board, which his son Oliver would also join in 1926. It may be that he preferred the life of a country squire and amateur historian to that of a businessman, but he certainly timed his move well. The twenty-year boom in brewing, on which Watney's had risen to prosperity, peaked in 1898, the year of the merger; 1899 saw a spate of bankruptcies among publicans which left brewers throughout the country heavily indebted, and a slump in the trade ensued, which would continue until the Great War.

When he bought Cornbury Vernon Watney was 40 years old. In 1891 he had married Lady Margaret Wallop, daughter of the 5th Earl of Portsmouth. The Wallops were an old aristocratic family, and Lady Margaret numbered the Earls of Carnarvon, Pembroke, Southampton and Tankerville among her forbears; but her father, christened Isaac Newton after another distinguished relative, preferred a fairly simple life and had refused both a Marquessate and the Garter from Mr Gladstone. He was a staunch Liberal, as were his sons, three of whom would eventually inherit the Earldom. Though they had little direct involvement in party politics, the Watneys' connections and doubtless sympathies were Liberal, and their time at Cornbury marks a break with its otherwise exclusively Tory traditions. Sir Edward Grey, Foreign Secretary at the outbreak of the First World War, was godfather to the Watneys' younger daughter Silvia, and later became a trustee of the Cornbury Estate. In 1911 his private secretary Charles Lyell, a young Liberal M.P., married the elder daughter, Rosalind.

Vernon Watney quickly set about his own alterations, employing one of the more distinguished architects of the time, John Belcher. Belcher is best known for public buildings (Colchester Town Hall), and department stores (Mappin and Webb, Whiteleys), but he also had experience in domestic architecture, having built Pangbourne Tower (later the Nautical College) in Berkshire, and enlarged Stowell Park in Gloucestershire for Lord Eldon. According to the *Dictionary of National Biography*, his work represents the approach of architecture to the Arts and Crafts Movement: he had been a founder member of the Art Workers Guild, and would soon (1904) become President of the R.I.B.A.

Du Cros' additions, the tower and the portico, were soon demolished, and the Clarendon Wing restored to its original state. Cornbury had always lacked a grand entrance, at which guests could be received directly from their carriages – Watney thought this was why Mrs Delany, back in the eighteenth century, had called it 'unfinished'. Du Cros had tried to solve the problem by adding a portico to the Clarendon Wing, but Belcher came

Great Hall by John Belcher, 1902.

up with a more discreet solution, which would better preserve the integrity of the historic house. The stable yard was transformed into an entrance court, from which a colonnaded porch led to a marble staircase and corridor, and finally to a new Great Hall in the inner angle of the Danby and Clarendon wings. This was two stories high and panelled in oak, with first floor arcaded galleries on two sides. These were approached by an oak

Portico by John Belcher, 1902.

staircase with tapestry-hung walls. The curved plasterwork ceiling, with cartouches at each end, was based on the ceiling of the Stone Hall designed for Danby in the 1630s. Such a large central Hall had become fashionable in late Victorian times, as it provided a social area that was free from the formalities of the Drawing Room. Men could come in from hunting or shooting and chat there in their muddy clothes, and they could also smoke even if women were present.

The Drawing Room and Dining Room were also redesigned, and extended by the removal of partition walls. The Drawing Room was deco-rated with carved pilasters, cornice and chimney-piece in cedar-wood, with an ornamental plaster ceiling. The Dining Room was given white-painted wood panelling and chimney-piece; the earlier ceiling and fluted Ionic columns were retained, and two more columns added. The Library was fitted with partly glazed oak bookshelves, and part of the old cellar in the Danby wing converted into a bookstore, connected with the Library by a new stair.

Outside, Belcher paved the terrace in front of the Clarendon wing, and built a pergola and rose garden at the northern end. The ends of the terrace were marked by wide pedestals with lead vases and groups of amorini. Beyond the lawn facing the Danby wing an 'Italian' flower garden was laid out with a water-channel running down the centre. He also built a new main entrance, with a pair of lodges and wrought-iron gates. For the lodges

The Dining Room.

stone was taken from the Buckleap Quarry, which had had been used for building the main house in the seventeenth century.

Finally, Watney employed Belcher to restore the tiny All Saints Church in Shorthampton, a short distance from Ranger's Lodge. It was during this restoration that the medieval wall paintings for which Shorthampton is famous were discovered. In the twentieth century Shorthampton would come to replace Finstock as the burial place for Cornbury's owners.

Like Harvey du Cros, Watney became an energetic patron of local activities. In Charlbury alone he was President of the Cricket and Football Clubs, of the Flower Show and Horticultural Society, and the Rifle Club. For some years he continued the annual meetings of the manorial court, which now took place at the White Hart and were followed by a good dinner, doubtless lubricated by an ample supply of Watney's Ale. Education, however, was his main interest: he was elected Chairman of the Managers of the new County School when it opened in 1903, and bought

The Drawing Room.

a plot of land next to the School to build a master's house. He was also Chairman of the County Education Committee from 1908 to 1914, and was an active figure in the public life of Oxfordshire. Before moving to Cornbury he had been a member of the London County Council, and a Wiltshire J.P. Now he joined the Oxfordshire Bench, and was a County Alderman from 1905 and High Sheriff in 1908. From 1918 to 1928 he was Chairman of the County Finance Committee, and in 1927 Vice-Chairman of the County Council. He served for many years on the councils of the Oxfordshire Territorial Force Association, and the Institute for Agricultural Economics at Oxford University. He was also a Radcliffe Trustee, a Deputy Lieutenant, and a Fellow of the Society of Antiquaries.

Lady Margaret, too, embarked on the career of local good works that marked her whole life at Cornbury. Within a month of arriving she had recruited and paid for a full-time nurse to work in the Charlbury and Cornbury district. Later she set up the Charlbury and District Nursing Association, and continued for years to organise various fund-raising activities to support it – rummage sales, concerts and fetes. In 1910 she started a Red Cross Society, which organised first-aid classes, initially for women only, but later for men as well.

But the Watneys also lived the traditional life of wealthy country gentry. The Heythrop Hunt was welcome to meet at Cornbury, and pheasant shoots were a regular social occasion. The first shooting party took place within days of their arrival, in November 1901, and one of the guests was General Sir Redvers Buller, recently returned from the South African War. (The General was Lady Margaret's cousin, and his nephew would marry the Watneys' younger daughter Silvia.) A committee of patriotic locals was formed to give him a fitting welcome, and the Charlbury Fire Brigade paraded in his honour. Later visitors included Sir Edward Grey, Lady Margaret's nephew John Christie, 'an erratic shot who once peppered a beater,' who later founded Glyndebourne Opera; and in 1914 Edward Prince of Wales, who is said to have been rebuked by Watney for turning up late for a shoot.

The years before the First World War saw the final flowering of English Country House life, and Cornbury was no exception. The naturalist W.D.Campbell, whose father was Head Gardener, spent his childhood there, and later described what it took to support this splendid and privileged existence.

> The estate where my father went to work must have been the major employer next to agriculture. Apart from butler, footmen, hallboy, housemaids, scullery maids, cooks, housekeeper and chauffeur, there was a groom and night-watchman. In the four acres of walled garden, the glasshouses produced tomatoes, bananas, peaches, pawpaws, figs and melons. Of the fourteen men under my father three were 'bothy-men', apprentice professional gardeners who lived in the bothy on the edge of the garden. In addition there were foresters, carters, masons, stone-wallers, hedgers and ditchers, sawyers, carpenters, gamekeepers, painters and decorators and even a full-time mole-catcher. The estate must have provided work for over 100 local craftsmen and labourers.

Campbell also records the clearing of the ponds on the Newell Stream. Two of them, the Trout Lake and Lake Superior, had been cleared of weed and coarse fish, and stocked with trout for fly-fishing. The pebbly streams flowing into the ponds provided ideal spawning conditions. But coarse fish

The Italian Garden.

The Pergola.

The Entrance Lodges.

found their way back in, and the trout suffered from the attentions of pike. Periodical restocking was needed, but first the weeds and coarse fish had to be cleared out again. 'The almost solid surface of weeds was cleared by a team on either side of the pool pulling a series of huge knives linked together, so that the weeds floated to the gridded sluice whence they were removed.' The fish were then shared out between the workers.

Another of Campbell's memories is of how, as a boy, he had been sent by his father up to the House to show Watney an unusual bird that had been caught in the fruit netting in the kitchen gardens. The squire and the small boy looked through bird books in the Library, and Watney noticed the boy's intelligent interest. The following day the postman brought two large and expensive bird books to the Campbell home. This episode reveals an imaginative and generous man, and helps explain why he was respected and admired by all those who worked for him. He was always concerned for his staff, and every Christmas there was a special service for them all, and their families, in the Chapel, followed by a party in the Stone Hall, with a huge Christmas tree, and individual presents for all the children.

But perhaps Watney is most memorable for his interest in the history of the estate he had bought, and the researches which led to his publication of *Cornbury and the Forest of Wychwood* in 1910. His love of history predated his purchase of Cornbury: he had previously rented the great

Above: The kitchen garden and greenhouses. Below: bananas in a greenhouse.

Elizabethan mansion of Littlecote in Wiltshire, and had written a book about the house and its owners which is a precursor of *Cornbury and the Forest of Wychwood*. Both books were published privately by Hatchards of Piccadilly. Watney's name does not appear anywhere in *Littlecote*; its Preface is signed modestly 'The Compiler', and it was as a 'compiler' that he described himself in the later work. As far as we know, he was the first

Vernon Watney in 1916, and Lady Margaret Watney in the 1920s.

owner of Cornbury to concern himself with its past, and he delighted in how, through Lady Margaret, he could trace a connection with so many of his predecessors. He named the bedrooms after them – the Clarendon Room, the Brydges Room, the de Langley Room, and so on. He accumulated a library that would have been the envy of a university history department, and must have given up much of his first ten years at Cornbury to his research.

Once his *magnum opus* on Cornbury and Wychwood was complete, he set about cataloguing his library and picture collection. The latter, divided between Cornbury and his London home in Berkeley Square, included works by Botticelli, Bronzino, Caravaggio and Tintoretto, Holbein and Franz Hals, Constable, Reynolds and Romney. There were also portraits connected with Cornbury's past: the first Earl of Clarendon by Jordaens, his daughter Anne Duchess of York, by Lely, and his granddaughter Mary II by Honthorst. Finally he compiled a set of pedigrees for his wife's family, the Wallops, which were published in four volumes, The Wallop Family and Their Ancestry, in 1928. 'With gratitude for more than 36 years of happy married life,' Vernon wrote in the Preface, 'these volumes are dedicated to a member of that family whose ancestry is herein recorded.' It was dated on St. Margaret's Day, 10th June 1927.

In 1919 the novelist John Buchan bought the Manor House at Elsfield and became a frequent visitor, bringing his children over for picnics in the Forest. He shared Watney's love of the Oxfordshire countryside and its historical associations, and when Watney gave him a copy of *Cornbury and the Forest of Wychwood*, it inspired him to write *Midwinter*, which was published in 1923. The book tells the story of a Highland Jacobite officer, Alastair Maclean, and his travels through England during the failed rebellion of 1745. In the second chapter he visits Cornbury where he encounters, not only Lord Cornbury and his sister Kitty, Duchess of Queensbury, but also the young Samuel Johnson. Much of the detail is taken from Mrs Delany's account of her visits in the 1740s, but also shows his personal knowledge of the geography of the House. Buchan and Watney loved both the English countryside, and the Scottish Highlands, where Watney owned a large estate in Sutherland. These shared loyalties are referred to in the dedication of *Midwinter* to Vernon Watney:

> We two confess twin loyalties –
> Wychwood beneath the April skies
> Is yours, and many a scented road,
> That winds in June by Evenlode.
> Not less when autumn fires the brake,
> Yours the deep heath by Fannich's lake,
> The corries where the dun deer roar
> And eagles wheel above Sgurr Mór.
> So I, who love with equal mind
> The southern sun, the northern wind,
> The lilied lowland water-mead
> And the grey hills that cradle Tweed,
> Bring you this tale which haply tries
> To intertwine our loyalties.

A later Buchan novel has the title *Witch Wood*, but this was set in Scotland. However, in 1931 he returned to the real Wychwood with *The Blanket of the Dark*, a tale set in the reign of Henry VIII, about a young heir of the Plantagenet kings who has been brought up secretly in Leafield, and tries in vain to recover his lost heritage.

The First World War would have had a serious effect on the life of the Estate, as many of its workers joined the army, but it gave Lady Margaret in particular a new outlet for social action. Within a week of its outbreak she was organising sewing parties to provide clothes for troops and hospitals. The following year they sent a parcel of comforts to every Charlbury soldier serving at the front. Throughout the War she was an active President of the local Red Cross. Vernon meanwhile ensured that the latest war news was displayed in the local Post Office, and presided over recruiting meetings. In 1915 a recruiting party from the Oxfordshire Regiment camped in the Park, and he gave a patriotic speech at the Town Hall after a film show.

The immediate post-war period saw the founding of a branch of the Women's Institute in Charlbury, and Lady Margaret again played a very active role as its President. Every summer its members were invited to tea at Cornbury, given a tour of the House, and a talk from Vernon about some aspect of its history. Neighbouring W.I. branches were also invited, and as many as 300 ladies enjoyed tea in the Stone Hall or the Riding School. Lady Margaret presided over Christmas Parties, and the younger members of the family played their part, providing entertainment in the form of playlets or music. She also embroidered a banner, presented to the branch in 1922, and now displayed in the Charlbury Museum. She did not treat her post as an honorary one, but actively presided over the monthly meetings of the branch, except when the family went to Scotland every summer for deer-stalking.

After the War Vernon continued with his usual round of local duties, adding to them the Presidency of the Charlbury Fire Brigade in 1926. He had promised to pay half the cost of a new Fire Engine, if the other half could be raised locally. This was the normal Watney approach to local charity, much of which went unrecorded. As John Kibble wrote in 1927, 'The present Lord of the Manor has been generous in gifts to the town...and there has been no "blowing of trumpets or beating of cymbals" about it.' In 1926 when coal was almost unobtainable because of the 8-month miners' strike, he distributed loads of firewood from the estate at the cost of carriage only.

It was during their annual visit to Scotland, in August 1928, that Vernon Watney suddenly died. He was out on a shoot, his ghillie pointed out a deer, he raised his gun, and fell dead from a heart attack. His body was brought back to Cornbury, where it rested overnight in the Chapel, before the burial the next day at Shorthampton. As the funeral was taking place, a memorial service was held simultaneously in Charlbury Church, to allow those who had benefited so much from his presence at Cornbury to pay their last respects. All the estate workers were left £9 in his will, the equivalent of a month's wages.

The estate now passed to the 26-year-old Oliver Vernon Watney, known to family and friends as 'Togo'. A tall, stooping man, he suffered from chronic tuberculosis, and so was inevitably a less active, more retiring man than his father. But he took just as seriously his responsibilities as a leading Oxfordshire landowner. He continued to support local charities and other activities, on two conditions – that local people should raise fifty per cent of the sum needed, and that his involvement should not be made public. In the 1930s he gave land in Finstock for the building of council houses, now known as Watney Cottages, and in 1946 sold land to the village at well below the market price, for use as a playing field.

The Watneys' close neighbours, in a new house at South Lawn, were Lord Redesdale and his daughters, the famous Mitford sisters. In 1928 Oliver became engaged to Pamela, the most domestically inclined of the family. It is said that his father had strongly encouraged the match, but that after Vernon's death Lady Margaret, less happy at the thought of a crowd of sparkling, argumentative Mitford in-laws, persuaded him to rethink. After taking a cruise the following year for the sake of his health – he had been too ill to attend his father's funeral – he and Pamela agreed to break off the engagement. 'What a let-off in the way of brother-in-laws!' wrote Nancy Mitford to her brother, but there must have been relief in both families. Pamela returned her engagement ring, but kept the replica of Alfred's Jewel from the Ashmolean Museum that Oliver had given her. She passed it to her sister Unity, who later presented it to Hitler.

In 1934 Oliver married Christina Nelson, whose father, Thomas Nelson, had been killed at Arras in 1917. He was an old Oxford friend of John Buchan, who had worked with him in the famous family publishing firm Thomas Nelson and Co. before the War. The wedding took place in St Margaret's Westminster, with the Archbishop of Canterbury officiating. Over forty tenants and staff from Cornbury were included in the invitation – a characteristic Watney touch. Shortly afterwards Lady Margaret moved to Hatherop, near Fairford, but she returned on frequent visits, and retained her Presidency of the Charlbury Women's Institute until her death

Oliver Watney, aged 4.

in 1943. Her daughter-in-law took over the Chairmanship of the Nursing Association in 1938, and in the mid-forties was for a while President of the W.I., but was less active than Lady Margaret had been.

Oliver's most notable public work was as a magistrate. He was appointed a J.P. in 1929, at the age of 26, and remained on the bench until his death in 1966, when he was Chairman of the Chipping Norton bench and also a member of the county magistrates committee and appeals committee. At that time he was described as 'an exceptional chairman. Although a somewhat retiring man, he did a tremendous amount of work behind the scenes. We recognised in him the true qualities that have made lay magistrates such a part of the British constitution. He was full of common sense and completely fair-minded. He took his duties with complete seriousness.' Like his father, he served as High Sheriff, in 1937, and became a Deputy Lieutenant in 1961. He took over his father's place as President of the Fire Brigade Committee, and the Charlbury Flower Show and Horticultural Society. He also remained a director of the family firm, Watney, Combe & Reid, and was a Governor of Guys Hospital. His main leisure activities were shooting and racing, and he ran his own stud at Cornbury.

The Second World War brought more upheaval than the First. Part of the House was taken over by a group of some 40 War Office officials in September 1940, and from December 1941 the Park was used as a military repair depot. Areas visible from the House, looking down to the lakes and the Vista gate, were kept clear, but the remainder was filled up with lorries, jeeps, and military vehicles of every description, the trees providing cover against enemy aircraft. They stayed until the end of 1947, when a sale of 5000 vehicles and trailers was ordered by the Ministry of Supply. The wrought-iron gates were put in store, and replaced by wooden ones. A concrete road was built parallel to the main drive to protect the latter, and gates and guard posts erected all round. The Vista Gate was especially strictly guarded, to prevent any vehicles entering the Forest. The Grand Vista itself, and Newell Plain, were ploughed up and turned over to corn.

Many of the estate staff were called up, while the gardens were kept up by girls from the Land Army. Those who remained formed a Cornbury unit of the Home Guard, and Oliver became its Captain. He was fiercely protective of the estate, and especially of the families living there; any hint of misbehaviour by the soldiers towards them brought instant complaints to their superiors. An American hospital was built at Finstock Heath, and the recuperating soldiers would walk down in their pyjamas to the lakes; when they started bringing rifles to shoot at the squirrels Oliver soon put a stop to it. Another American unit visited the lakes for a while to practice water purification techniques, erected their tents by the Newell stream, and set up gun emplacements all round to protect themselves.

After the War the Park was restored to its earlier state, and the whole area round the lakes cleared and kept in immaculate order. In 1955 Wychwood Forest, together with the Newell stream, was declared a National Nature Reserve (now a Site of Special Scientific Interest). The end of coppicing and the removal of the deer and cattle had created a high forest with a wide

Oliver Watney in the 1950s.

variety of trees. The official description of the Wychwood SSSI calls it:

> the largest continuous area of ancient broadleaved forest in
> Oxfordshire. It is mostly oak-ash woodland with an understorey of
> hawthorn, hazel and field maple... The woodland structure and
> composition is varied and uneven-aged with a wide variety of stan-
> dard trees and understorey shrubs. There is a stand of beech high
> forest and several species of hard and softwood trees have been
> planted in the wood in recent decades. There is an unusual example
> of forest with maple occurring as standards over an understorey of
> hawthorn or hazel coppice. Other frequent understorey shrubs are

sallow, privet, spindle, buckthorn, wild cherry and dogwood, with occasional rowan, crab-apple, guelder rose and holly. The climbing shrubs honeysuckle and traveller's joy are widespread.

For the Watneys life at Cornbury continued much as before. Oliver had a particularly severe bout of TB in the late 1940s, and from then on would make annual trips to the south of France and the West Indies. He kept up the family hunting lodge in Scotland, and weekend parties would gather at Cornbury throughout the pheasant shooting season. But one weekend in December was always kept free, so that the staff could do their Christmas shopping. The number employed was still comparable to that of Edwardian times. In 1950 the Watneys were served by a Butler, a Valet, a Cook, a Housekeeper, four living-in maids and three from outside, and an odd-job man. There was a chauffeur, and a 'Park keeper', whose task was to keep the Park tidy, clearing up fallen wood and so on. There was a night-watchman, who was on duty from 10 p.m. to 6 a.m., who had to record his presence at three separate 'boxes' each half-hour throughout the night. There were ten gardeners, an Estate foreman, two carpenters, two painters, four stonemasons and three odd-job men. There were also thirteen forest workers, some of whom were Italians on two-year contracts.

Then there were the gamekeepers, to service the annual ritual of pheasant shooting. The Head Gamekeeper, Charlie Barnes, spoke about his work to Mollie Harris in the 1980s. He had started work for the Watneys in 1926, and had seven to nine keepers under him. During the shooting season dozens of poachers crept in from nearby villages, and three keepers would be on duty each night to protect the pheasants. They met at Waterman's Lodge and would hide up in trees where the poachers were most likely to come. One noted poacher from Charlbury was, unexpectedly, often employed as a beater – this way the keeper could at least keep an eye on him. Another keeper's duty was shooting vermin – rabbits, cats, squirrels, foxes, magpies, jackdaws and carrion crows; weasels, stoats and moles would be trapped. Foxes, moles and weasels would be skinned at once, and their skins dried and sold. During the hatching season Barnes went around the neighbourhood finding broody hens to rent for half a crown each, to sit on the pheasant eggs until they hatched. Then they would stay with the chicks until they were old enough to be left, and the hens were returned to their owners.

The outside workers were paid five shillings a week above the statutory wage for estate workers, and also had an extra week's annual holiday. Their perks included two loads of wood each year, and fresh milk delivered to the door at half price. As in Vernon's day, at Christmas there would be a service in the Chapel, and a Christmas party in the Stone Hall for all their families, with a large Christmas tree and presents for the children. On retirement they were granted a free house for life and a pension of two days' pay per week. They were all left a legacy in Oliver's will, of a week's wages for each year of service. And there were other thoughtful touches – when *Country Life* published an article on Cornbury by Christopher Hussey in 1950, all the staff were given an offprint.

But this paternalistic community was becoming something of an anachronism, and in Oliver Watney's later years the modern world made encroachments he found it hard to deal with. A demand by some estate staff for union rates of pay caused ill-feeling and division, and then there was the matter of rights of way. Watney did not wish to keep the public at a distance – for two hours every Thursday morning local people could walk though Cornbury Park, and on Thursday afternoons the inhabitants of Finstock were allowed to enter the Forest to gather firewood through the Pound gate. He also took a relaxed attitude towards people walking through the Forest, but did not want this established as a matter of right. On Palm Sundays, when villagers walked through the Forest to the Iron Spring, estate staff were stationed at all turnings off the path to prevent anyone straying. In the 1950s, the County Council drew up a definitive map of rights of way, and Watney objected to any paths through the Forest being included. A claim for such rights could have been made by the Parish Council; but the Civil Parish of Cornbury and Wychwood had (and has) only a few dozen inhabitants, most of whom were tenants or employees of the Cornbury Estate. There was no Council, only a parish meeting, whose chairman was Watney himself, and the clerk his farm manager. When the County Council held an enquiry into footpaths on the Estate, it took place in the Estate office, and not surprisingly no rights of way were registered. In later years this would lead to angry disputes between the Estate and bodies like the Ramblers' Association.

Oliver and Christina had no children, and on his death in 1966 everything was left to his niece Helen Buller. Death duties made it impossible to keep the estate in the family, and she had no choice but to sell. The contents of the house were disposed of in a six-day sale in March 1967, while the pictures were sold separately at Christies in June. The *Oxford Times* called it one of the most important private collections in the world, and the auctioneers treated it appropriately, mounting a closely guarded security operation over several weeks to move them to London for the sale. 'I cannot reveal how the pictures were removed,' said the agent to the Estate, 'but Christies' methods certainly surprised me.'

The Estate was bought by Robin Cayzer, 2nd Lord Rotherwick, who moved from Bletchingdon Park nearby. Like previous owners, he made his own alterations to Cornbury House. Belcher's 1902 additions – the court-yard entrance and portico – were removed, and the Hall had a first floor inserted – a historical echo of what Hugh May had done to Danby's Great Hall in the 17th Century. The architect was Sir Philip Jebb, and the interior was redesigned by the London decorators Colefax and Fowler.

When Vernon Watney concluded his *Cornbury and the Forest of Wychwood* in 1910 he celebrated with lyricism a natural environment where the changes were merely seasonal:

In the winter, there stand out against the sky the graceful outlines of the trees; in the spring, the young branches are tinted by the bloom of the rising sap, while the blackthorn is covered with snow-white blossoms; soon the wild cherry is in full flower, and as the violets and the primroses and the cowslips fade, the bluebells herald the approach of summer, when the hawthorn fills with its fragrance the forest, wherein are spread the rock-rose and the ground-ivy; and in autumn the wonderful colours of the bracken and of the beech leaves shroud in their beauty the fading season of the year.

To many wild birds Wychwood and Cornbury still afford a sanctuary; the three woodpeckers are here, and here a cormorant was lately found; here sings the nightingale, and here the cries of the owls and the flight of duck break the silence of the winter nights; hither come the crossbill and the heron, and here are the nesting places of the kingfisher, of the woodcock and of the summer-snipe.

The rooks keep watch over the house at Cornbury, and the fallow deer feed round it, and in the forest there live (and die) the dark-necked pheasant and the rabbit(both of which the Romans are said to have brought with them to Britain), and here crawls that most ancient inhabitant of our island, the edible snail.

His Edwardian world seemed secure and unchanging, and having looked back over the long succession of previous occupants he could entrust Cornbury 'with confidence to the liberal rivalry of their successors.'

Nearly a hundred years later we are more conscious of change than stability. Everywhere commercial imperatives have transformed country estates. At Cornbury the shooting and fishing have become businesses. The roe and sika deer in the Park have to share its beauties with Game Fairs, Horse Trials, Caravan Club and Ford Fiesta rallies. Hugh May's stables have been converted into high-quality office accommodation, and a Business Park has been created out of old farm buildings at Southill. The great beech avenue has gone, but has been replaced, and this like other new planting is still following Evelyn's seventeenth century design.

A new awareness of Wychwood Forest has come with the founding in 1997 of the Wychwood Project. This brings together landowners, local authorities and public bodies, schools and local communities, with the aim of improving the countryside, increasing its biodiversity, and building up a much fuller understanding of the history of the area and its special identity. The Project encourages the planting of new woodlands, and trains volunteers in traditional skills like hedge-laying and dry-stone walling. It covers the whole of the Norman Royal Hunting Forest, and the hope is that by 2086, a thousand years after Domesday, a mature Wychwood Forest should again exist in West Oxfordshire. This revived Wychwood Forest, if the Project's aims are achieved, will be the result of free collaboration between local government, landowners, and local people – a welcome if somewhat ironic development in the history of a Forest which was seen on its creation by William I as an act of oppression, and whose later history was largely one of corruption, mismanagement and ecological deterioration.

Notes

1 Oxfordshire County Archive, Misc. B.T. II/I; Apl/III/iii/7
2 Oxfordshire County Archive, 0170/D/14

Sources

The main source is Vernon J. Watney, *Cornbury and the Forest of Wychwood*, 1910.

Material from the Oxfordshire County Archive has been footnoted. I have also made use of various items in the Charlbury Museum, especially a file of extracts from the *Oxford Times*; and of articles by W.D. Campbell, some of which are to be published in *W.D. Campbell: Naturalist and Teacher*, edited by Mary Jackson (Wychwood Press, 2003).

Other books and articles that have proved helpful are:

Adam Smith, Janet, *John Buchan*, 1965

Arkell, W.J., 'The Building Stones of Blenheim Palace, Cornbury Park, Glympton Park and Heythrop House, Oxfordshire', in *Oxoniensia*, XIII, 1948

Belcher, C., 'On the Reclaiming of Waste Lands as instanced in Wichwood Forest', *Journal of the Royal Agricultural Society of England*, Vol. XXIV, 1863

Bindoff, S.T., *The House of Commons 1509-1558*, 1982

Bonomi, Patricia U., *The Lord Cornbury Scandal: the Politics of Reputation in British America*, 1998

Buchan, John, *Midwinter*, 1923
-       *The Blanket of the Dark*, 1931

Calvertt, John Simpson, *Rain and Ruin: Diary of a Leafield Farmer 1875-1900*, ed. Celia Miller, 1983

Chandler, Keith, *'Ribbons, Bells, and Squeaking Fiddles'* – the Social History of Morris Dancing in the English South Midlands 1660-1910, 1993
-       'Wychwood Forest: A Study of the Effects of Enclosure on the Occupational Structure of a Group of Leafield Workers', in *Oxfordshire Local History*, Vol.3 No.5, 1990

Churchill, Viscount, *Be All My Sins Remembered*, 1964

Colvin, H.M., *A Biographical Dictionary of British Architects*, (3rd ed.), 1995

Copeland, Tim, *Iron Age and Roman Wychwood*, 2002

Cruickshanks, Eveline, *Political Untouchables: The Tories and the '45*, 1979

Eddershaw, David, *The Story of the Oxfordshire Yeomanry 1798-1998*, 1998

Emery, Frank, 'The Transformation of Wychwood: Some Fresh Evidence', in *Oxfordshire Local History*, II, 1984

Fawcett, William, *The Heythrop Hunt*, c.1935

Freeman, Michael, 'Whichwood Forest Oxfordshire: An Episode in its Recent Environmental History', in *Agricultural History Review*, Vol. XLV (ii), 1997
-   'Plebs or Predators? Deer Stealing in Whichwood Forest Oxfordshire in the Eighteenth and Nineteenth Centuries', in *Social History*, Vol. XXI (i), 1996

Gelling, Margaret, *The Place-Names of Oxfordshire*, 1953

Gibson, Robin, *Catalogue of Portraits in the Collection of the Earl of Clarendon*, 1977

Grant, Raymond, *The Royal Forests of England*, 1991

Grimaldi, Stacey, *Report upon the Rights of the Crown in the Forest of Whichwood in the County of Oxford*, 1838 (MS. in Oxfordshire County Archive)

Groves, Muriel, *The History of Shipton-under-Wychwood*, 1934

Guinness, Jonathan, *The House of Mitford*, 1984

Hammersley, George, 'The Revival of the Forest Laws under Charles I', in *History*, XLV, 1960

Harris, Mollie, *Wychwood: the Secret Cotswold Forest*, 1991

Hasler, P.W., *The House of Commons 1558-1603*, 1981

Henderson, M. Sturge, *Three Centuries in North Oxfordshire*, 1903

Hill, Oliver and Cornforth, John, *English Country Houses: Caroline 1625-1685*, 1966

Howkins, Alun, *Whitsun in 19th Century Oxfordshire*, (History Workshop Pamphlet 8), 1973

Hussey, Christopher, 'Cornbury Park, Oxfordshire', in *Country Life*, Sept. 1950

Hutchinson, G.T., *The Heythrop Hunt*, 1935

Keighley, Charles (ed.), *Discovering Wychwood*, 2000

Kibble, John, *Charlbury and its Nine Hamlets*, 1927
-   *Wychwood Forest and its Border Places*, 1928
-   *Charming Charlbury*, 1930

Lewis, Lady Teresa, *Lives of the Friends and Contemporaries of Lord Chancellor Clarendon*, 1852

McNamara, F.N., 'King John's Palace at Little Langley, Oxfordshire', in *The Berks, Bucks and Oxon Archaeological Journal*, 1899

Marshall, Edward, *The Early History of Woodstock Manor*, 1873

Mole, Robert, *An Evenlode Trio*, 1993 (typescript in Charlbury Museum)

Newman, John, 'Hugh May, Clarendon and Cornbury', in John Bold and Edward Chaney (edd.), *English Architecture Public and Private: Essays for Kerry Downes*, 1993

Ollard, Richard, *Lord Clarendon and his Friends*, 1987

O'Neil, B.H.StJ., 'A Civil War Battery at Cornbury, Oxfordshire', in *Oxoniensia*, X, 1945

Orr, J., *Agriculture in Oxfordshire*, 1916

Oxfordshire and District Folklore Society Annual Record, 1954

Pettit, Philip A.J., *The Royal Forests of Northamptonshire: A Study in their Economy 1558-1714,* Northamptonshire Record Society Vol. XXIII, 1968

Pevsner, Nikolaus, and Sherwood, Jennifer, *The Buildings of England, Oxfordshire,* 1974

Pope, Alexander, *Correspondence,* ed. George Shirburn, 1956

Raphael, Sandra et al., *Of Oxfordshire Gardens,* 1982

Schumer, Beryl, *Wychwood: the Evolution of a Wooded Landscape,* 1999

Sedgwick, Romney (ed.), T*he House of Commons 1715-1754,* 1970

Serocold, W.P.(ed.), *The Story of Watneys,* 1949

Sparrow, W. Shaw, *The British Home of Today,* 1904

Thompson, E.P., *Customs in Common,* 1991

Thorne, P.G., *The House of Commons 1790-1820,* 1986

Tiller, Kate, 'The Transformation of Wychwood', in *Oxfordshire Local History,* I, 1983

Victoria County History of Oxfordshire, Vols. II, X and XII

Walpole, Horace, *Correspondence,* ed.W.S.Lewis

Watney, Vernon J., *A Catalogue of Portraits and Miniatures at Cornbury and 11 Berkeley Square,* 1915

-     *The Wallop Family and their Ancestry,* 4 vols., 1928

Wickham-Steed, Violet, *The Great Days of Wychwood Forest (1154-1306),* (typescript in the Centre for Oxfordshire Studies)

-     'Hermitages and Chapels in Wychwood Forest', in *Top. Oxon.,* X, 1963

Woodward, Frank, *Oxfordshire Parks,* c.1982

Young, Arthur, *General View of the Agriculture of Oxfordshire,* 1813 (rep. 1969)

Young, C.R., *The Royal Forests of Medieval England,* 1979

State papers:

Journals of the House of Commons Vol. XLVII, Jan 31 1792 – Nov 15 1792

Report of the Select Committee of the Commissioners of Woods, Forests & Land Revenues of the Crown, 1848

An Act for Disafforesting the Forest of Whichwood, 16 & 17 Victoria, C.36 (1853)

Index

Other books from the Wychwood Press

Iron Age and Roman Wychwood
The Land of Satavacus and Bellicia
Tim Copeland

One day, in the early centuries of the present era, two individuals carved their names on a pottery syrinx, a set of clay pipes. These were subsequently found in the excavation of Shakenoak Roman villa near Witney in Oxfordshire in the 1960s and though damaged, a male name, SATAVACUS, was quite clear. The second name had been truncated by a break but reads BELLICIA..., and belongs to a female.

What is significant is that, besides possibly identifying a lover and his lass, these names are both from the pre-Roman Iron Age tradition – even though the pipes were found in the debris of a building that was dated to almost two hundred years after the Roman invasion. The names demonstrate continuity between the people living in Wychwood before the arrival of the Romans and those who worked the land for centuries after that event.

The Iron Age and Roman periods in Wychwood still have an impact on the area today. The pattern of the roads, the parish boundaries, the sites of villages and the distribution of vegetation have evolved in part from decisions taken to meet the inhabitants' needs in the period from 800 BC to 400 AD. Local people's routes to work, their leisurely footpath walks, even some of the local place names, may have originated in that period.

This profusely illustrated book is about the evidence, or lack of it, in Wychwood for the Iron Age and Roman periods, including hill forts, Akeman Street, Grim's ditch, Roman villas, religious sites, and much besides. It is also about the evolution of our understanding of that period of the past. It examines the work of significant individuals who have constructed a dynamic past characterised by increasing knowledge and reflecting the concerns of the periods in which their explorations took place.

Tim Copeland is Head of the International Centre for Heritage Education at the University of Gloucester, Chairman of the Council of Europe's Cultural Heritage Expert Committee and a Fellow of the Society of Antiquaries. His recent and forthcoming publications include work for the Council of Europe, the National Trust, the Royal Fine Art Commission and English Heritage.

£12 pbk 144pp 1 902279 14 X

May Day to Mummers
Folklore and Traditional Customs in Oxfordshire
Christine Bloxham

A fascinating, detailed and often highly entertaining account of the customs and festivities that took place in Oxfordshire before the days of mass media and multinational entertainment.

Customs dovetailed neatly into the farming year. There was recreational activity and celebration coupled with practices relating to fertility of both crops and people that harked back to pre-Christian times: their evolution is evidence of changing religious beliefs and social patterns. Traditions could also provide an opportunity for making money, sometimes for a good cause (such as the whit ales that raised money for the parish) and at others for private gain (as when morris dancers toured the countryside or children made May garlands to display).

Among hundreds of different customs described, often in the words of contemporary sources from the last 400 years, particular mention should be made of the very many customs associated with May, the strong morris tradition that survives in certain towns and villages, the mock mayor-making in Abingdon, Banbury, Oxford and Woodstock, the Burford dragon ceremony, various traditions of beating the bounds, the mummers plays that are still performed in some places, bun throwing in Abingdon, and the ritual of 'hunting the mallard' that takes place once a century at All Souls College, Oxford. The book includes the text of two mummers' plays (from Islip, dating from about 1780, and Westcott Barton, recorded in 1870) and a Christmas miracle play collected in Thame in 1853.

Includes many rare and unusual photographs, as well as photographs of modern revivals of ancient customs.

Christine Bloxham is a former assistant keeper of antiquities at the Oxfordshire Museum. Her previous books include *The World of Flora Thompson*, (1998). She has been collecting local folklore for thirty years.

£12.99 pbk 320pp 1 902279 11 5

MY THREE HATS

The autobiography of a schoolgirl at Milham Ford, a member of Stonesfield Silver Band, and a keen Oxford United supporter

Dorothy Calcutt

"I have always thought that my life – starting in a poor but striving family in a rural community in 1920 – saw more twentieth-century changes than most.

In those days our milk, meat, bread and groceries were all delivered by horse in a variety of vehicles. Combe had no amenities; an urgent message was sent by telegram and delivered by hand. The cricket team still took pigeons to send home their progress. As the crow flies the village was nine miles from the centre of Oxford, nearly six miles from Witney, and two-and-a-half miles from Woodstock (though almost twice that by road!).

All children went to the village school until the age of fourteen. The cane was in frequent use.

The average family had ten or more children, yet they lived in rented or tied two-bedroom cottages.

Girls were forced into private service to give more room both at the table and in bed. Boys were considered an asset. Girls did not anticipate careers, men expected to finance the family and females accepted domination by males.»

So Dorothy Calcutt begins her story. Her early life revolves around the family's tiny cottage, their smallholding and her parents' simple Methodist faith. In 1931 she wins a scholarship to Milham Ford School in Oxford, and begins the tortuous journeys by bicycle and train from Combe to the school on The Plain. A country girl in a school of sophisticated middle-class city girls, and her accent and family life the object of open ridicule, Dorothy's experiences both good and bad remain firmly imprinted in her memory for life. And she still has the hat!

From Milham Ford Dorothy goes into teaching, cycling the seven miles to the school in Kiddington. In 1944 she marries Frank and children follow. All become musical enthusiasts, playing in the Stonesfield Silver Band. Another hat! As the children grow up, Dorothy and Frank find time for football, and become avid supporters of Oxford United. Dorothy acquires her third hat…

This tale of personal adventure, triumph and tragedy, social change and rural transformation, recalls the experiences of millions of country people struggling to adapt to the rapid changes of the twentieth century.

£8 pbk   112 pages, illustrated   1 902279 25 8

THE SALT OF THE EARTH

Diary of a poor family in Woodstock, 1900

Dorothy Calcutt

One year in the life of a large family living on the edge of the Blenheim Palace estate in Woodstock, Oxfordshire in 1900. The author's mother, Dora, told her daughter many tales of her childhood at the turn of the century, and this book is based on those stories.

Includes contemporary photographs of the people and places in the story.

£8 pbk   120pp   1 902279 06 9

Born in a Stable

The true story of John Ashton, illegitimate son of a Northumberland nobleman and an Oxfordshire village barmaid

Dorothy Calcutt

Leo has inherited the family mansion in Northumberland, but is frustrated in his desire to have a son to continue the name and inherit his estate. To 'prove' his manhood, he is unfaithful to his wife. The barmaid at an inn in the Oxfordshire village of Long Hanborough (Emma, the author's great-grandmother) bears him a son, John.

This book tells the story of Leo's ambitions, of John's birth in extreme poverty in a farmyard stable, and of his upbringing and occasional meetings with his father. The events take place half a century before those in *The Salt of the Earth*.   £7.50 pbk   1 902279 13 1   80pp

Discovering Wychwood

An illustrated history and guide

Charles Keighley (Editor)

The history and guide for visitors and residents alike, and the only book of its kind.

Includes about 100 photographs and line drawings, and two colour plates

£8.99 pbk   168pp   1 902279 09 3

Charming Charlbury, its Nine Hamlets and Chipping Norton

John Kibble

John Kibble published *Charlbury and its Nine Hamlets* in 1927 and *Charming Charlbury* in 1930. Re-issued for the first time in a single volume, these two books give a tantalising and unique insight into two hundred years of life in this quiet corner of the Cotswolds, conveyed in the memories, stories and records of the people Kibble knew and met.

£10 pbk   224pp   1 902279 05 0

A History of Charlbury

Lois Hey

With a study of the town's geology by Professor Geoffrey Walton

The history of the Cotswold town of Charlbury, from pre-history to the present day. Illustrated with many historical photographs from local collections. Includes chapters on dissenters, schools, pubs and the gloving industry.

£8.99 pbk   144 pp   1 902279 03 4

The Forest that Sailed Away

Poems by Elizabeth Birchall

Illustrations by Amanda Henriques

This beautifully illustrated homage to ancient woodlands and to the sailors whose ships were built from them draws on the mythic meaning of individual trees and original accounts of historic voyages, and closes with poems celebrating renewed sensitivity to ecological balance and diversity.

£7.99 pbk　64pp　1 902279 10 7

'Walk Humble, My Son'

Growing up in Ascott-under-Wychwood, 1918–1939

Eric R. Moss

Including My Personal Memories, *by Doris Warner*

Eric Moss's graphic and moving account of life between the wars in a poor family that can trace its ancestors back to the seventeenth century. Doris Warner won first prize in a county competition for her *Memories*, which include both world wars and their impact on Ascott life.

Illustrated with many historic photographs.

£8 pbk　144pp　1 902279 07 7

Wychwood: The evolution of a wooded landscape

Beryl Schumer

Foreword by Harold Fox, Head of the Department of English Local History, Leicester University

The history of the woodland, showing exactly how extensive the tree cover was in the Norman period, and which settlements were already in existence. It traces later developments which have created the landscape of today.

£7.50 pbk　128pp　1 902279 02 6

Wychwood Forest and its Border Places

John Kibble

Foreword by Roy Townsend

Like his father and grandfather before him, John Kibble was a stonemason. Born in 1865, his memories are of people who lived and worked in, and remembered the life of, the forest villages in the 1700s and 1800s.

£7.50 pbk　128pp　1 902279 00 X

Winchcombe

A history of the Cotswold borough

D. N. Donaldson

The story of life in Winchcombe from earliest times. The book is illustrated with many old photographs, drawings and plans.

£14.95 pbk　272 pp　1 902279 12 3